THE
ORIGINAL
BLUE-BEARD

THE HISTORY OF
GILLES DE RETZ

By

THOMAS WILSON

First published in 1899

Read & Co.

Copyright © 2020 Read & Co. History

This edition is published by Read & Co. History,
an imprint of Read & Co.

This book is copyright and may not be reproduced or copied in any
way without the express permission of the publisher in writing.

British Library Cataloguing-in-Publication Data
A catalogue record for this book is available
from the British Library.

Read & Co. is part of Read Books Ltd.
For more information visit
www.readandcobooks.co.uk

To my
DEAR WIFE

The Companion of my Travels
While the Material for this Volume was Gathered
The Partner of my Many Joys
The Sharer of my Few Sorrows
This Volume is Affectionately Dedicated

T. W.

CONTENTS

ILLUSTRATIONS

GILLES DE RAIS (OR RETZ)

1404 – 1440

Marshal of France and the central figure of a 15th-century cause célébre, whose name is associated with the story of Bluebeard, was the son of Guy de Montmorency-Laval, the adopted son and heir of Jeanne de Rais and of Marie de Craon.

He was born at Macbecoul in September or October 1404, and, being early left an orphan, was educated by his maternal grandfather, lean de Craon. Chief among his great possessions was the barony of Rais (erected in the 16th century into the peerage-duchy of Retz), south of the Loire, on the marches of Brittany.

He joined the party of the Montforts, supporting Jean V. of Brittany against the rival house of Penthiévre. He helped to release Duke John from Olivier de Blois, count of Penthiévre, who had taken him prisoner by craft, and was rewarded by extensive grants of land, which were subsequently commuted by the Breton parliament for money payments.

In 1420, after other projects of marriage had fallen through, in two cases by the death of the bride, he married Katherine of Thouars, a great heiress in Brittany, La Vendée and Poitou. In 1426 he raised seven companies of men-at-arms, and began active warfare against the English under Artus de Richemont, the newly made constable of France.

He had already built up a military reputation when he was chosen to accompany joan of Arc to Orleans. He continued to be her special protector, fighting by her side at Orleans, and afterwards at Targeau and Patay. He had advocated further measures against the English on the Loire before carrying out the coronation of Charles VII. at Reims. On the 17th of July he was made marshal of France at Reims, and after the assault on Paris he was granted the right to bear the arms of France as a border to his shield, a privilege that was, however, never ratihed. In the winter he was in Normandy, at Louviers, whether with a view to the release of Joan, then a prisoner at Rouen, cannot be stated. Meanwhile his fortune was disappearing, although he had been one of the richest men in France. He had expended great sums in the king's service, and he maintained a court of knights, squires, heralds and priests, more suited to royal than baronial rank.

He kept open house, was a munificent patron of literature and of music, and his library contained many valuable works, he himself being a skilled illuminator and binder. He also indulged a passion for the stage. At the chief festivals he gave performances of mysteries and moralities, and it has been asserted that the *Mystére de la Passion*, acted at Angers in 1420, was staged by him in honour of his own marriage. The original draft of the *Mystery of Orleans* was probably written under his direction, and contains much detail which may be well accounted for by his intimate acquaintance with the Maid. In his financial difficulties he began to alienate his lands, selling his estates for small sums. These proceedings provided his heirs with material for lawsuits for many years. Among those who profited by his prodigality were the duke of Brittany, and his chancellor, Jean de Malestroit, bishop of Nantes, but in 1436 his kinsfolk appealed to Charles VII., who proclaimed further sales to be illegal.

Jean V. refused to acknowledge the king's right to promulgate a decree of this kind in Brittany, and replied by making Gilles de Rais lieutenant of Brittany and by acknowledging him as a brother-in-arms. Gilles hoped to redeem his fortunes by alchemy; he also spent large sums on necromancers, who engaged to raise the devil for his assistance. On the other hand he sought to guarantee himself from evil consequences by extravagant charity and a splendid celebration of the rites of the church. The abominable practices of which he was really guilty seem not to have been suspected by his equals or superiors, though he had many accomplices, and his criminality was suspected by the peasantry. His wife finally left him in 1434-35, and may possibly have become acquainted with his doings, and when his brother René de la Suze seized Champtocé, all traces of his crimes had not been removed, but family considerations no doubt imposed silence. His servants kidnapped children, generally boys, on his behalf, and these he tortured and murdered. The number of his victims was stated in the ecclesiastical trial to have been 140, and larger figures are quoted. The amazing impunity which he enjoyed was brought to an end in 1440, when he was imprudent enough to come into conflict with the church by an act of violence which involved sacrilege and infringement of clerical immunity.

He had sold Saint Étienne de Malemort to the duke of Brittany's treasurer, Geffroi le Ferron. In the course of a quarrel over the delivery of the property to this man's brother, Jean le Ferron, Gilles seized Jean, who was in clerical orders, in church, and imprisoned him. He then proceeded to defy the duke, but was reconciled to him by Richemont. In the autumn, however, he was arrested and cited before the bishop of Nantes on various charges, the chief of which were heresy and murder. With the latter count the ecclesiastical court was incompetent to deal, and on the 8th of October Gilles refused to accept its jurisdiction. Terrified by excommunication, however, he acknowledged the evidence of the witnesses, and by confession he secured absolution. He had been pronounced guilty of apostasy and heresy by the inquisitor, and of vice and sacrilege by the bishop. A detailed confession was extracted by the threat of torture on the 21st of October. A separate and parallel inquiry was made by Pierre de l'Hôpital, president of the Breton parliament, by whose sentence he was hanged (not burned alive as is sometimes stated), on the 26th of October 1440, with two of his accomplices. In view of his own repeated confessions it seems impossible to doubt his guilt, but the numerous irregularities of the proceedings, the fact that his necromancer Prelati and other of his chief accomplices went unpunished, taken together with the financial interest of Jean V. in his ruin, have left a certain mystery over a trial, which, with the exception of the process of Joan of Arc, was the most famous in 15th-century France.

His name is connected with the tale of Bluebeard in local tradition at Machecoul, Tiffauges, Pornic and Chéméré, though the similarity between the two histories is at best vague. The records of the trial are preserved in the Bibliothéque Nationale in Paris, at Nantes and elsewhere.

A BIOGRAPHY FROM
1911 *Encyclopædia Britannica, Volume* 22

INTRODUCTION

THE story of Bluebeard has become a classic in infantile mythical (folk-lore) literature wherever the English and French languages are spoken. Rev. Dr. Shahan suggests its possible existence in earlier languages and more distant countries (see p. xiv.). The story is more or less mythical. While it does not follow history with any pretence of fidelity, it has come to be recognised by the historians and literati of France as representing the life of Gilles de Retz (or Rais), a soldier of Brittany in the first half of the fifteenth century. He was of noble birth, was possessed of much riches, was the lord of many manors, had a certain genius and ability, made some reputation as a soldier at an extremely early age, fought with Joan of Arc, and was Marshal of France. At the close of these wars he retired to his estates in Brittany, and, in connection with an Italian magician, he entered upon a search for the Elixir of Youth and the Philosopher's Stone. Together they became possessed by the idea that the foundation of this elixir should be the blood of infants or maidens, and, using the almost unbridled power incident to a great man (at that early date) in that wild country, they abducted many maidens and children, who were carried to some one of his castles and slain. Suspicion was finally directed toward him; he was arrested, tried, convicted, sentenced to death, and executed at the city of Nantes, October 27, 1440, at the early age of thirty-six years.

The author of this volume was sent, in 1882, to the good city of Nantes as United States Consul. While resident there he entered upon the investigation which resulted in this volume. He obtained access to the original records of the trial in the archives of the department, and made a photographic copy of one of its manuscript Latin pages which is shown in its proper place. The trial of Gilles de Retz took place in the château of Nantes, sentence was pronounced at the Place Bouffay, and he was executed on the Prairie de la Madeleine, the exact locality being now occupied by the Hospital of St. Anne. The author procured photographs and drawings of some of these localities, which will appear in this volume.

* * * * *

Monsieur Charles Perrault was the author of the story of *Bluebeard*. He was born at Paris, January 12, 1628. His father was an advocate, originally from Tours. He was the youngest of four brothers: the oldest, Peter, was destined for the Bar, but became the Receiver-General of Finances under Louis XIV. and his Prime Minister Colbert, though he afterwards fell out of favour and died in poverty; Claude studied medicine; and Nicholas, theology. Charles was taken up by Colbert and made Superintendent of Public Buildings throughout the kingdom. While in this position, the erection of the Observatory and the reconstruction and completion of the Palais du Louvre were determined upon. Plans for these buildings were to be decided by competition, and the renown of the name of Perrault is greatly increased by the fact that Charles's brother Claude, although educated as a doctor of medicine and not as an architect, designed plans which, after much discussion and investigation, extending even to Rome, were finally adopted by the King and his Minister. Charles Perrault became a member of the Academy—one of the "Immortal Forty." He introduced many improvements into their methods, the principal of which was for securing the attendance of members, and a continuance of, and devotion to, the work of preparing the great French Dictionary. An episode in his life, covering several years, was his poem of *Le Siècle de Louis le Grand* and the parallel between the ancients and moderns, which produced a discussion

12

among the most brilliant writers of France. Boileau, Racine, La Fontaine, Longpierre, Buet, Arnauld, and other illustrious champions took up the cudgels against Perrault and Fontanelle, and in favour of the ancient classic heroes.

In 1662, Perrault retired from his office in the Public Buildings, selling his right therein to Monsieur de Blainville, a son-in-law of Colbert. Until his death, May, 16, 1703, he devoted himself to literature and to the education of his children, and this was probably the happiest portion of his life, for he loved to be in the bosom of his family. He wrote for the amusement of his children that which has now become the most celebrated of his writings, which has done more to perpetuate his name and fame, and by which he is better known than by the more pretentious and serious papers and poems,—the *Contes de Mère l'Oye* (Stories of Mother Goose). The first edition was published in 1697 under the name of his son, Perrault d'Armancourt, and dedicated to Mademoiselle Elizabeth Charlotte d'Orléans, the sister of the Duke of Chartres and the niece of Louis XIV. These Mother Goose stories were as follows: *Little Red Riding-Hood, The Fairies, Bluebeard, The Sleeping Beauty, Puss in Boots, Cinderella, Requet à la Houppe,* to which *Le Petit Poucet, The Adroit Princess,* and *The Ass's Skin* were afterwards added. There were still others in verse and fable translated. Perrault was more poet than prose writer—his serious works were in poetry: *Painting, The Apology for Women, The Century of Louis the Grand, Genius* (to Fontanelle), and *A Portrait of the Voice of Iris.* We, however, are interested alone in *Bluebeard.*[1]

Studious historians or astute critics may dispute Perrault's history of Bluebeard having been founded upon the life of Gilles de Retz, but the country people (the folk) of Brittany will simply smile at such erudition and continue in their former belief that Bluebeard represents a cruel, wicked man who lived here hundreds of years ago and who was executed for his many

1   See Appendix A.

13

crimes against humanity; and the old men and women and the nurses will repeat the story of Gilles de Retz under the name of Bluebeard,—sometimes how he abducted and murdered the children, and other times how he murdered his wives. In that country Gilles de Retz will always be known as Bluebeard, and we must accept their verdict as final.[2]

Rev. Dr. Shahan writes:

DEAR PROFESSOR WILSON:

I have looked through your interesting work with the greatest pleasure. It is just such a tale as I would delight in tracing through its strange genesis and stranger propaganda . . .

I wonder if the actual facts were not soon plaited back into ancient nursery tales of a kindred tone, and a fresh lease of life thus given to mythical narratives that would otherwise not have had strength enough to perpetuate themselves to our time, at least in such intensity and vitality.

I would suggest as complete a literature of the *Bluebeard* subject as possible2 and think perhaps it would be well to see what roots it had struck in German, Spanish, and Welsh soil,— fields always susceptible at that time to anything odd or romantic.

When I was a child how often I cried with Sister Anne on the high tower, and looked for the three specks out on the ocean "no bigger than the head of a pin." Thank God! their steeds always breasted the flood bravely and *arrived in time to save injured innocence.* Is not that the true origin of *Bluebeard*, in an age of chivalrous ideal, of strict theologico-popular views of justice and of feudal individualism?

The box of Pandora and the key of Bluebeard may have some relationship—CURIOSITY, irrepressible though dangerous, is its keynote, and I wonder if it does not all come from India, like those mediæval tales that Gaston Paris tells about, or if it is not

---

2   See Appendix B.

14

an old Gaelic myth, like that of *Balor-of-the-Mighty-Blows* so well translated by Standish O'Grady in his *Silva Gadelica* . . .

Yours very truly,

(*Signed*)
THOMAS J. SHAHAN.

*Château (Castle) of Nantes,
where Gilles was tried.—From the river Loire.*

BLUEBEARD

CHAPTER I

GILLES DE RETZ

THE original of Bluebeard in the Mother Goose story was Gilles de Rais (changed in 1581 to Retz), though he is sometimes called *Gilles de Laval* in history. Neither the date nor place of his birth is known with precision, but it took place in the autumn of 1404, probably at Machecoul, one of the family châteaux in the southern part of Brittany.

The ancestors of Gilles de Retz belonged to four noble and illustrious families in Brittany: 1. Laval, sometimes called Montmorency-Laval; 2. Rais (changed to Retz in 1581); 3. Machecoul; and 4. Craon. These families could trace their ancestry to the eleventh or twelfth centuries. Gilles's father was a Laval or Montmorency-Laval, named Guy; his grandfather was also Guy, and many of his ancestry bore the same surname. His grandmother was a sister of the great Du Guesclin; his great-grandmother was Joan, called *la Folle*, or "the Crazy."

The House of Rais in that day was represented by Joan la Sage (the Wise), 1371–1406. Being without heirs she, in 1400, by solemn act, adopted Guy de Laval, the father of Gilles, as her heir and successor. A legal impediment existed in an act of disinheritance which had been passed against Joan la Folle, the grandmother of Guy de Laval, and it required a special decree to enable Guy to accept the inheritance. This was finally done under the condition that he should abandon the name, arms, and escutcheon of the family of Laval, and bear those of Rais. But Joan la Sage afterwards repented of her choice and attempted, by act of May 14, 1402, to change her succession in favour of Catherine de Machecoul. This begat a suit-at-law, which was taken by appeal to the Parliament at Paris. By this time Jean de Craon had come to be the heir of his mother, Catherine de Machecoul. He had a daughter named Marie, and for the settlement of a contest which, it was feared with reason, might be interminable, it was agreed between the families, as it was between York and Lancaster, that the representatives of the two respective houses should be intermarried, and accordingly, in the spring of 1404, Guy de Laval (changed to be Guy de Rais) was married to Marie de Craon, and thus it was that Guy de Laval, the father of Gilles, became the heir and successor of Joan la Sage (of Rais), received her property, and took her name.

There has been some dispute among the historians of Brittany as to dates, but it is agreed that the contest at law between the two families was begun in 1402, was still found on the parliamentary records in 1403, and was settled by the marriage, which the best authorities agree took place February 5, 1404.

Guy de Laval (Rais) and Marie de Craon were the parents of Gilles de Rais, who was their first-born. His birth is believed to have taken place at the château of Machecoul during the last months of the year 1404. A doubt has been thrown over these dates, especially that of his birth, because of his extreme youth when he made his appearance in public affairs. If born at that time, he would appear to have been a Marshal of France at twenty-five years of age; but this was not impossible, and the weight of the evidence seems to favour the dates as given.

The parents of Gilles had another son, René de la Suze, but he seems to have made but little figure compared with his redoubtable brother. Guy de Laval, the father, died on the last

18

day of October, 1415, and the records show his last will and testament dated on the 28th and 29th of that month. He gave the tutelage of his sons to a distant cousin, John de Tournemine; but by some means not appearing, the maternal grandfather, Jean de Craon, took upon himself their guardianship. The mother, Marie, was remarried soon after the death of her husband, to Charles Desouville, the Lord of Villebon. The grandfather of Gilles and René seems to have been excessively indulgent and devoted to the children, and if he was old, he was of strong will, fiery temper, staunch patriotism, and obstinate disposition.

In 1417, when Gilles was but thirteen years old, he was engaged by his grandfather to Joan Peynel, the daughter of Foulques Peynel, the Lord of Hambuie and Briquebec; but the contract was voided by her death. In November, 1418, the grandfather made for him a second contract of marriage, this time with Beatrice de Rohan, the eldest daughter of Alain de Porhoet. The contract was signed at Vannes with great ceremony in the presence of an illustrious throng of Breton nobles. But this contract came to an end, as did the former, by the unfortunate death of the young lady. This double failure did not, however, discourage the doting grandfather. He immediately proceeded with his arrangements for a third contract, this time with Catherine de Thouars, the daughter of Miles de Thouars and Beatrice de Morgan, and this marriage was celebrated on the last day of November, 1420. The young wife, Catherine, brought to her husband, Gilles, the property of Tiffauges, Pouzauges, Savenay, Confolons, Chabenais, and others of minor importance. The first two mentioned were well provided with châteaux. The property and château of Machecoul came to Gilles through his mother's family, and the château and property of Champtocé came to him upon the death of his grandfather. This, with the fortune of his father, Guy de Laval, to which must be added that of the family of Rais left by Joan la Sage, made Gilles de Rais one of the richest barons of the province.

Under the conditions of the adolescence of Gilles de Retz, his education may be better imagined than described. Left at the age of eleven an orphan or a half-orphan, by the death of his father; the remarriage of his mother within a year thereafter; the contest of greater or less gravity over his guardianship, which ended in the success of his maternal grandfather, whose best recommendation for the position seems to have been his love for his grandchildren and his subsequent willingness to indulge them, and also his great desire to get them (especially the elder) married and off his hands, a proceeding which he conducted with such celerity that the young man was engaged three times with all pomp and formality, and finally married by the time he was sixteen years old: this would seem to afford but little time or opportunity to obtain an education, even under the best facilities, however studious and seriously inclined he might have been.

Education did not stand very high in the province of Brittany at this era. There was much excuse, especially for the nobles and barons of Brittany, for their lack of education. The profession of war seems to have been the highest recommendation, and the shortest, as well as the easiest and most agreeable, road to preferment. There is much to be said on the score of patriotism and the needs of the country, for, as will be seen farther on, it was an era of war, and Brittany was in the midst of it. The education in arms was almost inevitable; it had greater attraction for Gilles than books, arts, or sciences; and it appears that his grandfather allowed him to pursue his own wishes and desires without even an attempt at control. Gilles, during his trial, said: "In my youth I was allowed to go always according to my own sweet will." Nevertheless, he spoke three languages, Latin, French, and Breton, had some knowledge of chemistry, and it seems to be without question that he had a library, so well chosen as to be an object of commendation and attraction to highly educated persons. In the inventory of his effects, taken in 1436 and found among his records, is a receipt of Jean Montclair given to Jean Bouray, for a book a copy of Ovid's *Metamorphoses*, described to have been in parchment covered with leather-gilt, with copper clasps and locks of silver-gilt, with a crucifix of white silver on the back.

CHAPTER II

GILLES AS A SOLDIER
1420 – 1429

IN the condition of his country at that time, it was but natural that this handsome, impetuous, rich, and powerful baron should take up arms as his profession. France and England were in the midst of the Hundred Years' War. Brittany, Gilles's own duchy, had been since the death of John IV. engaged in a civil war over the succession. The family of Montforts (son of a younger son) had gained the victory over the Penthièvres and Blois (daughter of an elder son). Gilles's father and his family had fought on the side of Blois, but on his defeat they had made their peace with the victorious Duke.

When Gilles was about sixteen years old an incident occurred which renewed the civil war and swept him into its midst. The head of the Blois family, with his mother, the daughter of De Clisson, set a trap for John V. (De Montfort), Duke of Brittany, inviting him, under a flag of truce, to a friendly conference to be held at the castle of Champtoceaux. This conference was only a pretence, the flag of truce was violated, and John V. was entrapped and held prisoner. He was treated with great severity, bound in chains, and cast into a dungeon. This inhuman treatment on the part of the Blois and Penthièvres, being in violation of every principle held sacred by men and soldiers, aroused the indignation of the Bretons to a pitch beyond control. The peculiar interest of this to the present memoir is that, while the ancestral families of Gilles de Rais had always theretofore fought on the side of the Penthièvres and Blois, they now turned to the other side and took up for John V. of Montfort.

Du Guesclin, the uncle, and Brumor, the grandfather, of Gilles de Rais on his father's side, were now dead; but Jean de Craon, his grandfather on his mother's side, he who had been so indulgent a guardian, still lived, and on the 23d of February, 1420, a few months before the marriage of Gilles, they repaired to the town of Vannes, attending upon a session of the States-General, convoked in the absence of the Duke by his wife. Part of the ceremony of Gilles and his grandfather was the oath of allegiance for the deliverance of their prince: "We swear upon the cross to employ our bodies and our goods, and to enter into this quarrel for life and for death,"—and they signed it with their proper hands and sealed it with their seals. The war broke out anew. Alain de Rohan was made Lieutenant-General. An army of fifty thousand men volunteered and took the field under him. In the front rank, by the side of his grandfather, at the head of all the vassals of their united baronies, was Gilles de Retz. This army marched against Lamballe which capitulated, Guingamp, the same, and successively Jugon, Chateaulan, Broon, and finally against the château of Champtoceaux in which the Duke was incarcerated. This resisted the assault but was besieged and finally taken, the fortress demolished, and John V. was released and returned to Nantes where he was given a triumphal entry.

The Château de Clisson, the headquarters of the Penthièvre faction, was south of Nantes twenty kilometres, and in the immediate neighbourhood of the most extensive property of Gilles de Retz. In revenge for his adhesion to the Duke of Brittany, which Margaret de Clisson was pleased to call his treason to her side, she found it most convenient to raid and destroy the adjacent properties of Gilles de Retz. In reprisal, the Duchess of Brittany confiscated certain rights which Olivier, Count de Blois, had in or about the Château de Clisson, and transferred them to the family of Gilles, and this was ratified by the Duke after his release. Then, as he says, "In recognition of the good and loyal services of his cousins, of Suze and Rais," he gives to them all the lands of Olivier de Blois, formerly Count de Penthièvre, and of Charles his brother. This was afterwards compromised by the payment of a certain sum of money. Penthièvres, Blois, and Clisson were cited to appear before the States-General, at which Gilles and his grandfather assisted as counsellors; and, as an end of all things, the Parliament of Brittany declared the Penthièvres guilty of felony, treason, and *lèse-majesté*, condemned them to death, and deprived them in perpetuity of their name, arms, and all honour in Brittany; but they escaped to France.

This was the introduction of Gilles de Retz to the profession of arms and his first appearance as one of the lords of the country. He was at that time only sixteen years old, and immediately upon the conclusion of this campaign he was married to Catherine de Thouars.

France, at that epoch, was in danger of the fate which afterwards befell Poland. The duchy of Aquitaine, which comprised nearly all south-western France, had for its duke Edward III., King of England. The duchy of Burgundy had for its head Philip the Good, who was Count of Flanders and was stronger in his duchy than was the King of France in his kingdom. These two were banded together by a treaty, offensive and defensive, and they and their countries were then, and had been for nigh sixty years, carrying on war against France with the avowed determination of establishing the King of England on her throne. The Duke of Bedford, son-in-law of the Duke of Burgundy, was the English general commanding in France. The Count of Richemont, the second son of the Duke of Brittany, was also the son-in-law of the Duke of Burgundy. Thus these strong nobles, princes, and kings were allied against France. In the dukedom of Brittany the contending houses of Blois and Montfort had been aided, respectively, by the King of France and the King of England, and had accepted and supported an English army on Breton soil. We all know of the condition of the dukedom of Normandy; how, only a few hundred years earlier, William captured England at the battle of Hastings and established himself as her king. This process was now in danger of repetition, only with the conditions reversed, and France had then in prospect a worse fate than she ever had before or since.

Such was the condition of France at the time of the death of Charles VI., on October 21, 1422, when his son, Charles VII., came to the throne. Charles VII., was married to Mary of Anjou, the daughter of Yolande of Aragon, Queen of Sicily, the widow of Louis of Anjou; a woman of noble heart, great spirit and patriotism, and devoted to France. Yolande set herself, with all her beauty and diplomacy, to divide and break up this coterie of great noblemen who had organised themselves against the King, and to induce some of them to become supporters of France. On March 24, 1425, Yolande started for Brittany accompanied by sundry powerful seigneurs. Jean de Craon, grandfather of Gilles de Retz, was one of those approached, and his valiant services rendered to John V. of Brittany, in releasing him from the dungeon at Champtoceaux, gave him great and deserved influence.

Gilles de Retz had returned to his home after the defeat of the Blois party, and was residing there in the quiet and peace of his newly married life, when this new turn was made in the political kaleidoscope. A council of the States-General of Brittany was assembled at the city of Nantes, and Gilles was one of the seigneurs in attendance. Naturally, he would be one of the lieutenants of his grandfather, Jean de Craon, who had openly espoused the cause of the King of France, and who went into the council with the expressed desire to win the Duke of Brittany in that direction. The Assembly pronounced strongly in favour of the alliance with the King of France, and the month of September was fixed as the time, and the town of Saumur, midway between Nantes and Angers, was appointed as the place, for a conference between the Duke of Brittany and the King of France. The terms fixed by the Duke were the same as those laid down by the Duke of Burgundy—that was, the expulsion of the

Penthièvre and Blois families from the Court of France. The King consented, and thus gained the active aid of the Duke of Brittany and the moral support of the Duke of Burgundy.

The peace between the Duke of Brittany and the King of France brought its first great fruits in the offer to the King by the Count of Richemont, the brother of the Duke of Brittany, of his services against England, which was accepted, and he, the Count of Richmont, was made Constable of France. To him, probably more than to any other man, was France indebted for the final victory over England, and the establishment of France in her place among the nations of the world. Gilles de Retz, still with his grandfather, Jean de Craon, embraced the side of the King with ardour. He was rich and Charles was poor. He entered with spirit into all the pleasure and gayety of the Court. He became a pronounced favourite, and despite the subsequent defection or opposition of the Duke of Brittany, and the renunciation or withdrawal of favour from the Count of Richemont, Gilles de Retz and his grandfather remained indissolubly bound to Charles VII. and to France.

The first appearance of Gilles de Retz in the service of the King of France, or as a member of his Court, was September 8, 1425. He took service with the Breton troops and made his first essay as a soldier on the side of the King of France in the siege of Saint-Jean-de-Beuvron.

Gilles de Retz associated himself with Ambroise de Loré and the Baron Beaumanoir (the son or grandson of him who led the fight for Brittany in the *Combat de Trente*). These three attacked and captured the fortress of Rainefort in Anjou, which capitulated with terms that spared the English soldiers, but left to be punished the Frenchmen who had committed treason against their country. Ambroise de Loré sought to save them, but Gilles was firm in his decision that they should hang as traitors, and such was their fate. The château of Malicorne was attacked by the same three, and captured, or surrendered, on the same terms. The two friends, Beaumanoir and Gilles, held together in their undertakings; they were together at the siege of Montargis, which was conducted by Constable Richemont and La Hire.

It was at this siege that La Hire, about to make the assault, was asked to join with the rest in prayer to God for aid and safety in the coming fight; he had not much experience in religious vernacular, but he joined hands, and with the fervour of a bigot and the faith of a devotee said: "O God, I pray Thee to do for me to-day what Thou wouldst that I should do for Thee, were I God and Thou La Hire." In the assault which immediately followed, Gilles de Retz arrived at the top of the wall in advance of his soldiers. The first Englishman encountered was Captain Blackburn, the commander of the English forces, whom Gilles engaged in a hand-to-hand combat, killing him outright. On seeing their chief slain, the English soldiers threw down their arms and capitulated on the usual terms. This exploit was recognised by all his superiors, and covered the young soldier with glory. But the victories of the French in the north were not equal to those gained by the English in the south, who, having captured nearly all France, Paris included, advanced into the interior, until at last they appeared before Orleans and commenced its memorable siege.

Then, in 1429, came the brilliant meteor across the sky of France, Joan of Arc, the Maid of Orleans. Her visions at Domremy, her travels across France, passing safely through the lines of the enemy, her arrival at the castle of Chinon, her presentation to the King, her assault and capture of Orleans, are all matters of history. The theatre of her exploits in western France was not far distant from the barony and residence of Gilles de Retz. He was the kind of man to be captivated by the Maid of Orleans, and he became one of her most devoted followers. It is said that he received from the King orders to be captain in her escort, whether as its commander does not appear, but he was with her at Chinon, Poitiers, Blois, Orleans, Jargeau, Meung, Beaugency, and Patay.

On the occasion of the King's coronation at Rheims, Gilles

de Retz received the baton of Marshal of France. There is a question as to the date, but none as to the fact. Some authorities give the date as June 21, 1429; others, again, say that with other peers of France he was promoted on the day of the coronation of the King, July 17, 1429; still others assert it to have been in the month of September. It is explainable that all three of these dates are correct, for the King might well have announced, on the earliest date, that he was to be promoted to the rank of Marshal of France; the ceremony of installation may have taken place upon the occasion of the King's coronation, and yet the commission not have been signed, or recorded, until September. That he was an officer in high command upon that occasion, and in favour with the King, cannot be doubted.

The Kings of France, from Clovis, the first convert to Christianity, down to Louis XIV., were crowned in the cathedral at Rheims. There is a tradition that upon the crowning of King Clovis a white dove miraculously descended from Heaven and hovered over, if it did not alight upon, the King's head, bearing in its beak the *ampulla* containing the consecrated oil for his coronation. The latter was retained and became a holy emblem under the name of Sainte Ampoule, and was preserved in the Abbey of Saint Remy, near the cathedral at Rheims, until it was destroyed during the French Revolution. From Clovis to Louis XIV. it figured in the coronation of every king of France. At the coronation of Charles VII., Gilles de Retz as Marshal of France, Marshal Boussac, Admiral de Culan, and Lord Graville were the four nobles of France chosen as its escort and guard of honour. After the coronation, Gilles remained in the service in his former position of guard, or captain of the guard, of Joan of Arc. He accompanied her to Paris, which the English evacuated and left to the care of the Duke of Burgundy.

The capture of Joan at Compiègne took place May 20, 1430, and her execution May 30, 1431. There is no evidence reported of Gilles's presence during any of this time. There has been found among the records of the barony of Rais, a paper wherein he acknowledged a debt to "Roland Mauvoisin, Captain of Prinçay, the sum of *huitvingtes* [twenty-eight] crowns of gold, for the purchase of a horse, saddle, and bridle, promised to his dear and well beloved Michel Machafer, captain of a certain company, as soon as they arrived at Louviers, in order to engage said captain to come with him on this voyage." This paper was dated December 26, 1431, at Rouen, and is signed with his own proper hand.

Gilles's signature and rubric

NOTE.

The army service of the Baron de Retz, his relation to Joan of Arc, and his investiture as Marshal of France, are authenticated in sundry histories of France.

Monstrelet (vol. ii., p. 96) mentions him as a Marshal of France.

Michelet (vol. v., p. 71) mentions the Marshal de Retz as one of the Bretons who went to the aid of the city of Orleans.

Sismondi (*Histoire des Français*, vol. xiii., p. 124), speaking of the advent of Joan of Arc, says:

"Le Roi l'envoya à Blois, après de la petite armée qu'y rassemblaient les Marécheaux de Rais et de Saint Sevire, Ambroise de Loré et le sire de Goncourt."

In *Jeanne d'Arc*, by H. Wallon (Paris, 1860), the author says:

"Le Maréchall de Boussac et le seignieur de Rais, investés du Commandement y rentrent Ares—peu aprés, avec La Hire, Polon de Xaintrailles et tous ceux que devaient faire l'escort, 10 ou 12000 x hommes."

And again in *Jeanne d'Arc*, by Harriet Parr (London: 1866, vol. i. p. 91). "The captains appointed to command the exploration (to Orleans) were the Marshal de Boussac, the Marshal de Retz, and Louis de Culant, Admiral of France."

The extent of the relation of Gilles with the incident of Joan of Arc may be obtained by taking Quicherat's history of the *Process for the Condemnation and Rehabilitation of Joan of Arc* (5 vols., Paris, 1849) the references in the index under the title of "Gilles de Rais":

Rais (Gilles de Laval, sire de) present at the arrival of Joan before the King at the castle of Chinon, iv., 363, 407.

He accompanies her to Orleans, iii., 4; iv., 5, 41, 53, 213, 491; v., 290; vi., 12, 20.

His return to Blois, iv., 54, 56, 152, 155, 221, 222; v., 290.

He assists at the Council with Jacques Boucher, iv., 57, 158. Combat at the capture of St. Loup, iv., 6, 43; at the capture of St. Augustine, iv., 61, 158, 226; at the capture of Tourelles, iv., 44; v., 261.

His departure from Orleans with Joan, iv., 165.

Took part in the expedition of Jargeau, iv., 12; v., 108, 261.

Combat at Patay, iv., 238, 239, 319, 371, 419.

He goes to Rheims, vi., 69, 180, 248, 378.

He is escort of the Sainte Ampoule on the occasion of the coronation of the King, iv., 77, 185; v., 129.

Made Marshal of France, v., 129.

In command at Montepilloy, iv., 83, 193.

Is sent to Senlis, iv., 24.

Figures in the attack on Paris, iv., 26, 86, 87, 197, 199.

Opposes (makes war on) the false Jeanne d'Arc, v., 333.

The *Livres de Comptes*, the official accounts of the Royal Exchequer, mention Gilles de Retz in connection with Joan of Arc on sundry occasions.

The eighth account of Guillaume Chartiers, receiver-general of finance, published by Godfrey in *Histoire de Charles VII.* (p. 89).

To Messire Gilles de Rais, Councillor and Chamberlain of the king, Sire and Marshal of France, the sum of one thousand pounds that our lord the king by his letters patent of xxi juin (M) CCCCXX at-arms in the Company of Joan of Arc and the employment in her service preparing for the siege of Tarjean.

Paid by the city of Tours to John Colez *10 livres tournois* for having brought the good news of the capture of Orleans by *la pucelle* [Joan of Arc], *Mgr. de Rais et les gens de leur compagnie.*

CHAPTER III

_____

GILLE'S LIFE AT HOME IN BRITANNY
1430 – 1439

THERE are but two known portraits of Gilles de Retz. That in the palace at Versailles is purely imaginative, and was only made to complete the series of the Marshals of France. It is not known by whom or at what time the other was made. In 1438, Gilles was thirty-five years old, tall, handsome, and well formed. He showed in his face, figure, and in every movement, his pride and spirit. He had a high, rather than broad, forehead; his nose was prominent and slightly aquiline; the nostrils were large and thin, and, on occasions of anger, spread and quivered in an interesting and threatening manner. His lips were rather thin but well coloured, and had a tinge of delicate and refined sensuality.

Like many of the Breton race, his complexion was fair, his eyes large and blue, and his eyebrows and lashes long and black. His hair was also long and black, and beard the same. It was soft and silky, and with its raven blackness became shiny, giving it a tinge of blue-black, which may have served as a foundation for his pseudonym in that country. His neck was neither too short, too long, nor yet too large, but seemed a column full of nervous strength, calculated to support solidly and well his head and brain, with whatever of pride, audacity, and confidence it might have. His shoulders were square, his body long, his waist small, while the bust and hips were large and fairly placed upon the muscular legs, which stood straight under him, giving his body firm support. His fingers were long and tapering, his hands small, and their fair complexion, when brought in contact with his velvet costume and lace ruffles, showed them to good advantage. Thus, he had the physical appearance of an athlete trained in all the exercises of the body; of much strength, a good walker, a good rider, and capable of any feat at arms.

Michelet (*Hist. de France*, vol. v., pp. 208–213) describes Gilles as of "*bon entendment, belle personne et bonne façon, lettré de plus, et appréciant fort ce qui parlaient avec élégance la langue latine.*"

Lemire says (p. 39) that Gilles, when he appeared before the Court, was dressed in pantaloons, skin-tight, after the fashion of the day, and shirt and vest, all of white wool, with boots also white. Over this was a doublet of pearl-grey silk embroidered with gold, with a hood of ermine; a sash of scarlet about his waist which supported a poniard with red velvet scabbard. He wore his military and seigniorial medals and orders, and about his neck a chain of gold with a reliquary. From the latter he never parted.

How much of this description is actual and how much imaginary will probably never be known; but in the attractiveness of his person and manner, Gilles de Retz compared with the best of his race in that country, and the foregoing might have been a fairly truthful representation. He seems the model of a gentleman of his time; his life being divided between the chase, war, and his adventures. He had beauty, force, riches, and occupied the highest rank among the nobility of his province. To him, nature and fortune had been blindly prodigal in their gifts.

On Gilles's return from service in the army of France, after the murder of Joan of Arc, he retired to his château, dwelling alternately at Machecoul and Tiffauges, with an occasional visit to his Hôtel de la Suze in Nantes. He engaged in no serious business, but apparently resigned himself to domestic pleasures and happiness. He established himself in a princely fashion. The interiors of his châteaux were decorated in the most magnificent and luxurious manner possible. He maintained a small army, the members of which were in his own pay. He was passionately fond of music; he purchased instruments and organised all sorts of musical competitions and displays. He established a religious hierarchy, having as a member of his own household a pseudo bishop with a large retinue, and all the necessary paraphernalia, including rich vestments for his servants and expensive decorations for his chapels.

This luxurious, magnificent, expensive mode of living was carried on for so long a time, increasing to such an alarming extent, that his brother René presented a memoir or petition to the King, called in history *Mémoires des Héritiers*, wherein these expenditures and extravagances were set forth at as great length and with as much detail and redundant phrase as though it were a bill in equity. This memoir ended with the prayer that the King should pass a decree against Gilles, interdicting him from making sale, transfer, or alienation, or mortgaging or pledging any of his property. This process is not unknown to French law. Without having the law of primogeniture as in England, the heirs yet had certain rights which, consequent upon the death of Gilles, would accrue to them under the law of France, and thus it was that the King was prayed to take the necessary steps for the protection of the rights of the heirs. In this proceeding his brother, René de la Suze, seems to have been the principal and moving spirit, although he was afterwards aided and abetted by his cousin, Guy de Laval.

From the *Mémoires des Héritiers* we get a knowledge of the property of Gilles de Retz. The list of his lands, possessions, and income, with his family ancestry, through which he received them, was as follows:

From the house of Rais, left by Joan la Sage, first the title of Baron and then the rank of Dean of Barons in the duchy of Brittany, with its châteaux and dependencies in great number, of which the principal only are named—Machecoul, Saint-Étienne-de-Mer-Morte, Pornic, Prinçay (or Princé), Vue, Ile de Bouin, etc.

From the house of Montmorency-Laval, the original ancestry

of his father,—independent of his adoption by Joan la Sage,—the seigniories of Blaison, of Chemillé, of Fontaine-Milon, and of Grattecuisse in Anjou; of Ambrières, Saint-Aubin-de-Fosse-Louvain, province of Maine; and others in Brittany.

From the house of Craon, through his grandfather and his mother, the Hôtel de la Suze at Nantes; the seigniories and châteaux of Briollay, Champtocé, and Ingrandes, province of Anjou; of Sénéché, Loroux-Botereau, Bénate, Bourgneuf-en-Rais, Voulte, and others.

From his wife, on their marriage, Tiffauges, Pouzauges, Chabanais, Confolens, Châteaumorant, Savenay, Lombert, Grez-sur-Maine, with *"plusiers autres terres fort belles, et leurs dépendencies."*

The value of this immense property has been estimated at four and a half millions of francs, though this may be exaggerated. His personal property was valued at one time at a hundred thousand golden crowns, and his income was variously estimated from thirty to sixty thousand pounds per annum.

It was alleged that he had made sales and transfers of property in an improvident manner and to an unjustifiable extent, dissipating to that extent his patrimony, to the damage of his estate and the detriment of his heirs. These were given somewhat in detail in the *Mémoires*, etc., viz.:

To Gauthier de Brussac, Captain-at-arms, the
    towns and seigniories of Confolens, Chabanais,
    Châteaumorant, and Lombert;
To Jean de Marsille, the châtellenie, land, and
    seigniorie of Fontaine-Milon in Anjou;
To Messire William de la Jumelière, the château
    and lands of Blaison, of Chemillé, in Anjou;
To Hardouin de Bueil, Bishop of Angers, the land
    and seigniory of Grattecuisse, the châtellenie and
    château of Saveny, half the forest of Brecilien;

To Messire Guy de la Roche-Guyon, the château and
    lands of Motte-Achard, and of Maurière, in Poitou;
To Jean Malestroit, Bishop of Nantes (who was soon
    to be his judge), the château and lands of Prigné, of
    Vue, Bois-aux-Treaux in the parish of Saint-Michel-
    Sénéché, and *un grand nombre de terres situés dans
    le clos du pays de Rais pour une somme énorme*;
To William de Fresnière and Guillemot le Cesne, merchants
    of Angers, the lands and seigniories of Ambrières, Saint-
    Aubin-de-Fosse-Louvain in the province of Maine;
To Jean de Montecler, one of his men-at-arms,
    and to Guillemot le Cesne, aforesaid, the lands
    and seigniories of Voulte and Sénéché;
To Jean Rabateau, president of the parliament, the lands
    and seigniories of d'Auzence, de Cloué, and de Lignon;
To William (apothecary at Poitiers), Jean Ambert, and
    Jacques de l'Epine, the lands Brueil-Mangon-lez-Poitiers;
To Georges Tremoille, late favourite of the king, now in
    retirement, twelve hundred "reaux" of gold on the
    rents of Champtocé, to pay interest money on twelve
    thousand "reaux" of gold formerly borrowed from him;
To Perrinet Pain, bourgeois and merchant
    of Angers, much interest money on loans
    secured on his lands and seigniories;
To the Chapter of Notre Dame, Nantes,
    his superb Hôtel de la Suze;
To Jean le Ferron, Saint Étienne-de-Mer-Morte, etc., etc., etc.

During some period, most likely in his younger days
and before his services in the army, Gilles de Retz became
enamoured of the theatre. His taste in this luxury was in
the same extravagant style as the chapels, the bishop, and his
religious secretaries.

There have been many histories of the theatre and the drama
in France written by French historians. *Histoire du Théâtre en*

France, Paris, 1881, two volumes, Monsieur Petit de Julleville; *Histoire de la Société Française au Moyen Âge*, Paris, 1880, by Monsieur Rosières; *Mise en Scène des Mystères*, Paris, 1885, by M. Paulin, Paris; *Le Drame Chrétien*, by M. Marius Sepet; *Tableau de la Littérature au Moyen Âge*, by M. Villemain; *Histoire du Théâtre Français*, Paris, 1745 to 1749, fifteen volumes, by les Frères Parfaict; *Dictionnaire du XIXme Siècle*, by La Rousse; and there may be many others, but with them all, our understanding of the extravagance and expenditure, and the consequent elegance and richness attained by theatres in France during the period in which we are now interested, would be incomplete without a study of the life of Gilles de Retz. His love for the theatre manifested itself not simply in looking at the spectacle and hearing the play, but in organising, arranging, and presenting the plays of the time in theatres established and conducted by himself. Some of these presentations were in his own châteaux, but others were given in the neighbouring cities—Nantes, Angers, Blois, Orleans, and minor places in the provinces of Brittany, Maine, Anjou, Touraine, and Poitou.

One cause of his indulgence in theatrical display appears to have been the desire to make himself popular with the people. That he loved the theatre and its plays, and that they gave him pleasure, is not to be doubted, but after all, it is supposed that his ambition to shine among the people formed the real foundation.

The theatre had always been intended as a means of amusement. An attempt was made in France and the Latin countries during the fifteenth century, to combine in the theatre instruction of a religious kind with pleasure and amusement. This attempt was fostered by the clergy, and, in its execution, theatrical plays were performed in sundry chapels and sanctuaries. Whether the Passion Play at Oberammergau is a revival or continuation of this custom, is suggested but not decided. But such plays were common enough in the fifteenth century and met with favour in the Church. In its origin, this departure was exclusively religious, and was adopted by the Church as an ingenious and original continuation of the education of the people in the mysteries of the Christian religion. Originally, it employed only sacred topics, and used only terms taken from the ritual, or from the Bible, and was altogether in prose Latin.

With the lapse of time, the imagination of authors, and the progress of popular language, theatrical representations passed from the chapels and holy places to the public places, and the Latin language was superseded by the vulgar. The priests who had conducted the play gave way to laymen, and the liturgy of the drama was superseded by other compositions. While religious scenes were continued and religious thoughts were the principal inspiration, yet there came interruptions and lapses. Secular and historic pieces were put upon the boards. These were occasionally fixed together and played, first one and then another, without attempt at regularity or continuation, as we in the present day may have everything from tragedy to farce in the same season at the same theatre. In the fifteenth century the favourite representations were the "Mysteries" and next the "Moralities," and after these, dramas and farces. The former were religious or historic dramas, calculated as much for religious or historical instruction and entertainment as for pleasure and amusement. The Last Judgment, the Birth of Christ, the Baptism in Jordan, the Marriage in Cana, and other Mysteries in the life of Christ were presented, usually on holy days, at Christmas, Easter, Ascension Day, and Pentecost. In not a few cases the theatre was in the open air, and this custom has been kept up in Brittany and certain provinces in France to the present day. While there are regular theatre halls in the cities, yet throughout the country are travelling troupes of mountebanks, jugglers, conjurers, etc., with trained dogs and other animals, who, arriving at a small town in the afternoon, pitch their tents upon the market-place or any other open square which can be secured, advertise the play by beating of drums or ringing of bells, charge one sou for a stand-up admission, and two sous for admission and a seat. The stage is made by unrolling a strip of carpet upon the ground or pavement. And here will be performed the sublime tragedy, the touching drama, and the roaring farce.

In the fifteenth century the plays, especially the Mysteries, whether religious or historic, were elaborate and extensive. The scene of the play varied according to its necessity and so was changed from town to country, from open street to walled town, the audience and actors being moved with it, as in certain ancient Greek theatres. An immense amount of decoration was required, which, however, was not usually a painted canvas stretched upon a frame, representing the desired object; but these scenes were made of the real thing, and the decoration, especially of the streets and walls about, were of hangings, usually of tapestry, though in cases of need any gaily coloured stuffs, like coverlets, bed-spreads, table-cloths, or carpets would be pressed into service. This custom exists in Brittany to the present day. The author well remembers one of the holy days in August, 1882, when, visiting the village of Savenay near Nantes, which by chance was one of the seigniories of Gilles de Retz, he witnessed the decoration of the village. The well-to-do residents brought out their tapestries and hung them along the fronts of their houses and garden walls; the poorer people, their carpets and coverlets, or anything which helped to make a gay appearance; while in one particular residence a bolt of white cotton cloth was brought out and stretched along the wall, covering it for a distance of fifty or sixty yards. This kind of decoration is not uncommon, and even in Nantes and Angers a greater amount of tapestry may be seen on a single holy day than otherwise during a year's residence.

Where required by the action of the drama, the scenes were built in the fashion of scaffolds. In the Mystery of the Creation the lower scaffold represented the earth, while the second or upper represented the heavens. In the Last Judgment and the Resurrection it consisted of two great scaffolds, making three stones one above another, the upper one of which represented

Paradise, with God upon His throne, the Virgin, the Christ, the angels; all the holy things. The middle stage represented the earth with the mortals engaged in their everyday duties; while the lower one represented Sheol with the Prince of Darkness in command, and the demons, small and great, engaged in their supposed task of keeping up the fires and of stirring up the spirits of the damned. The description of all this interests us in its relation to Gilles de Retz only because of its extravagance and immense expenditure.

The historic Mystery was also a favourite. The Mystery of the Siege of Orleans appears to have been the most popular and the most frequently played. But there were others: the Passion of Metz, the Mystery of Paris, that of Saint Michel of Angers, of Saint Barbe. Gilles de Retz organised, equipped, and presented no less than ten of these Mysteries. They were long, too; the Moralities contained about twelve hundred verses; while the Mysteries had many thousand verses, that of the Siege of Orleans having twenty thousand five hundred and twenty-nine lines; and they not infrequently required an entire day in the performance. The presence and aid of five hundred persons were required on some of these grand occasions.

One of the first paragraphs in the chapter on the extravagant and ruinous folly of Gilles in the *Mémoire des Héritiers*, tells that the establishment, organisation, and equipment of these theatres and the performance of the plays was at the expense of Gilles. The succeeding paragraphs enlarge upon his immense and ruinous expenditures in this regard. The decoration, apparel, apparatus, the costumes of all the actors, were ordered by him. He required the best of everything, while the question of expense or even of value seemed as nothing. When he wanted them, he wanted them, and they were purchased at the asking price. Each person had his special costume according to his rôle and dignity; the beggar, the varlet, the huntsman, as well as the soldier, knight, and noble, the fair ladies, the saints in heaven, were all accoutred and equipped with stuffs of such richness as would magnify the greatness and power of the author and owner of it all, and gratify his inordinate ambition. Gold, silver, velvet, precious stones, rich armour, luxurious harness, fine embroidery, silken stuff, satin, and all the marvels of art in profusion. When the ornaments of the Church were required in any scene or play, there were copes, chasubles, dalmatics, albs, and all the ecclesiastical robes so rich and sumptuous. His ecclesiastical paraphernalia was at the command of the theatre.

The follies and ambition of Gilles not only required his theatrical costumes and property to be of the richest and most expensive stuffs, but in his maladministration they were bought at highest prices, payment frequently made with promises greatly increasing their cost. With all this, his pride was such that he never permitted the same dress to be worn twice; everything was required to be made anew for each representation, or for each series of representations. New costumes seem to have been his particular fad in that day, so that he could use the same terms which now appear in the playbills of the city—"entirely new and elegant costumes." Having been once used, they were thrown aside or sold at whatever could be gotten for them. This meant to buy at the highest price and sell at the lowest, a system which we well know produces financial ruin. His ambition and desire to please led him into foolish and useless expenditures. All his theatres and the plays rendered by him were free; the people who attended paid nothing. Gilles paid the expenses of the entire entertainment. Consequently, one can easily understand the statements made in the *Mémoirs* of the ruin wrought by these representations, the cost of each one being thirty, forty, and fifty thousand francs (six, eight, and ten thousand dollars).

Gilles's favourite play was the Mystery of the Siege of Orleans. Here he was not only actor but principal. It was a drama in verse though not in rhyme. It was based upon the events of that memorable siege. Quicherat says of it that its historic value is *nil*, not because the author has removed it from the domain of history, but for the contrary reason, that he was quite too near, both in space and time, to the events as they happened, and was, therefore, unable to take the rôle of historian, and make deductions. He could not form conclusions, nor announce principles: all that he did was to recount the actions and events as they happened day by day. He was a recorder, not an historian. The drama or poem was largely romance; while recounting the daily progress of the siege, it was not a veritable or trustworthy journal thereof. The words put into the mouths of the various actors were probably never spoken by them, certainly never were heard by the author. But they were the speech of the day; they were news gathered at the time and which might have appeared in the daily newspapers, if such things had then existed. It is because of their nearness to the events that they are not history. How long the Mystery of the Siege of Orleans continued to be represented in the theatre as a drama is immaterial.

One hundred and forty personages have been introduced upon the stage, not counting the groups of soldiers, peasants, citizens, musicians, etc. The Marshal de Retz figured in it as one of the prominent actors, in close relation to the King and to Joan of Arc. Not only is his name mentioned, but he himself had a speaking part and was present on the stage. Naturally he would take his own part and appear under his own name in the play; and this was both a compliment to his courage and ability as a soldier, and his versatility as an artist. While it kept him constantly before the people, it gave him an opportunity to gratify his ambition. It is useless to give any description of it, for it is simply the representation of the siege of Orleans written by one who, while he did not copy the journal, had it under his hand while writing the drama. Because it is in verse, it will not be practicable to translate much or any of it, but a few paragraphs will be given in which Gilles de Retz figured, and will be inserted (Appendix C) for the purpose of bringing out his part.

A description of one of these Mysteries has been given us by Monsieur Paul Saunière. Its presentation took place in the

Place Notre Dame before the Cathedral at Nantes, on May 21, 1439, under the direction, and at the expense, of Gilles de Retz. It was the Mystery of the Lord Jesus Christ and of the Virgin Mary. It was written by a young poet, Jean Lanoë, and Gilles de Retz is reported to have paid him the sum of ten golden crowns. Whether the story told by Saunière is absolute verity, is of slight consequence. There can be little doubt that it represents truthfully the custom of the period relating to such spectacles, and is a fair description thereof. Much of it is recognised as in accordance with habits and customs of that country in the present day.

All public proclamations and announcements by official authority in the provinces are made through the aid of either trumpet or drum, but in Brittany with the trumpet. The herald or other officer, when making an official sale, begins generally at the City Hall, makes the round of the city, sounding his trumpet at prominent places, calling the people together to hear his announcement, which he makes *viva voce*, and so passes on to the next place, repeating the performance. Lost children are cried in the same way, except that when done by a private individual a bell is used.

In the present case, the herald-at-arms was richly dressed in the livery of his master, the Baron de Retz, accompanied by a guard of four soldiers, or men-at-arms, who escorted him and kept the crowd at a distance while he blew a call on his trumpet; and then he made his announcement, which is given as follows:

"We, noble and powerful Baron, Gilles de Retz, Marshal of France, Lord of Champtocé, Tiffauges, Machecoul, Saint Étienne-de-Mer-Morte, Pornic, and other places, do by these presents make known, that by the express permission of the high and powerful Lord Seigneur, Jean de Malestroit, by the Grace of God and the Holy Father, the Bishop of Nantes, there will be given on the 21st day of the present month, at two o'clock afternoon, at the Place of Notre Dame, a presentation of a Mystery concerning the

44

life of our Lord and Saviour Jesus Christ, and of Madam, the Holy
Virgin, His Mother."

When the herald ceased, the soldiers closed up the circle
that had been made around him and prepared to escort him
to another place, while the crowd cried, "Liesse, Liesse, to the
Marshal—Liesse to our Lord Bishop!" The herald and his men-
at-arms departed and the crowd dispersed.

The locality of the presentation of this spectacle adjoined
the cathedral on its right as one stands facing it. This Mystery
had but a single scene, and required but a single stage. This
stage, intended for the use of the actors, was flanked on either
side by an alcove or balcony; that on the left, intended for the
high dignitaries of the Church and the city, the nobles, and
other persons of distinction was decorated with long and heavy
curtains of blue velvet bordered with gold, the upper portion
thereof being provided with rings to slide upon a curtain rod,
by which means the occupants of the alcove could be cut off
from the view of the multitude. This balcony bore the arms of
the archbishop and those of the city of Nantes. The balcony on
the opposite side of the alcove was arranged with curtains in the
same way, but it was draped with red velvet decorated with a
border of white velvet and gold braid and tassels. This balcony
bore two coats of arms, both belonging to the Baron de Retz—
one was the house of Retz itself, gold with *croix de sable*; the
other, that of Machecoul, *trois chevrons de gueules sur le champ
d'argent*. The stage for the actors formed the centre of the alcove,
but was brought to the front to enable the populace to see it, and
was decorated with red velvet bearing the coat of arms of the
city of Nantes.

As the hour for the spectacle approaches, the crowd gathers
in the place, and soon it is a mass of people, bourgeoisie and
peasantry, most of them wearing the peculiar costumes of
the country.

A street in Nantes—Ancient houses.

The archbishop with his suite could reach his balcony by a private way. The Baron de Retz occupied his hotel called Maison de la Suze in the Rue Notre Dame. This Maison de la Suze has been destroyed, and no representation of it is in existence. There are, however, many other of the ancient streets lined on either side with houses belonging, if not to that precise epoch, to the one immediately following, and as such may here be given with propriety as presenting a reasonably faithful idea of the city. Many of these houses are historic and have been occupied by persons of renown and distinction. Similar houses are to be seen in other towns of Brittany—Vannes, Quimper, Angers, Laval, Dinan. These houses are usually built of frames of wood with great beams and posts as shown, and not infrequently the principal beams across the front of the house bear a carved inscription. The author has seen these in Vannes and Auray, of which the following are samples:

PAX HVNC DOMVN ET OMNIBUS HABITAN
IRVS IN EA ICI JAN FOLLIART MA FAICT FAIRE
LAN 1560.

AV NOM DE DIEV, DIEV SOICT EN MES AFFAIRES.
YVES LEKME ET PERRINE LEBAR SA COMPAGNE
ONT FAICT FAIRE SE LOGIS EN IVING 1565.

Returning to the spectacle of the Mystery: The Baron de Retz passes out from his great double gates or doors which form the entrance to his Maison de la Suze, accompanied by his guards of honour, whose glittering armour reflects brilliantly the rays of the sun. With their halberts, they press back the crowd to make way for the Baron and his suite. By his side, and within easy reach, walks one of his men-at-arms, holding a casque upturned, more or less filled with coined money, of which the Baron occasionally takes a handful and scatters among the crowd, first on one side and then on the other. Arrived at the balcony intended for him, the guards of honour open their ranks, press back the crowd, take their station at the foot of the steps and along the front of the balcony, while the Baron, accompanied by his suite, among which were his chapel, as it is called, comprising his bishop and some thirty ecclesiastics of divers names and functions, mount the balcony and take their places, the Baron, of course, at the front and centre. It is said that his display of church and ecclesiastical dignitaries was unwarranted, that it had never been authorised by the Pope, that his Bishop had no ecclesiastical jurisdiction, nor was he lawfully entitled to perform the functions or support the dignity, and it was also said that his appearance in this character had always irritated, if it did not anger the Bishop of Nantes.

The description of this spectacle has not been preserved to us, though, as with the Mystery of Orleans, of which a few copies of the libretto have been preserved, this spectacle at Nantes excited the populace and aroused their enthusiasm, to which they gave vent with cries of joy and great huzzas. The dignitaries were present with many of their suite, in gorgeous dress and costumes, their men-at-arms with casque and cuirass, Damascene steel and shining halbert and scabbard. Their coats-of-mail were fire-gilt, and covered them from waist to knees; gloves and boots of red leather completed a brilliant and striking costume. The prelates, on the other hand, with their magnificent official robes of scarlet and gold and silver, with the curtains and hangings of such royal magnificence, all served as a background for the play of the Mystery which, being of the Infant Jesus and the Virgin Mary, excited the deep-seated religious fervour and enthusiasm of the people. They manifested their joy and enthusiasm in the usual way of crowds, but the principal share was devoted to the Baron de Retz. This was the pleasure reserved for him; this was the compensation for his great expenditure. It gratified his ambition, tickled his vanity, gave him pleasure, justified his expenditure, confirmed his extravagant habits, and led him farther in the course which ended in his ruin.

It would scarcely be possible at this late date, to obtain a more complete report of the prodigalities of Gilles de Retz than is furnished by the *Mémoires des Héritiers*, which, as it was sufficient for the King, should be sufficient for us; but there will occasionally crop out of the historical desert of this ancient time a record which, by giving information on a particular subject, lifts the veil from his life and gives us glimpses into certain extravagances, whereby we may imagine the result. One of these, lately found among the archives at Orleans, and contributed by M. Doinel, is a memorandum of a visit of Gilles to that city from September, 1434, to August, 1435. He was accompanied by his suite and retinue, military and ecclesiastic. His brother, René de la Suze, was with him, which was the only time they are shown to have been together, and, curiously enough, it must have been while the *Mémoires des Héritiers*, if not already presented, were being prepared, or at least contemplated; for the decree of the King was published within the next two years; yet no mention is made therein of René's presence on this trip.

Arrived at Orleans, Gilles de Retz installed himself, with his personal adjutants, at the Hôtel Croix d'Or (Golden Cross), while his suite and high officers with their respective retinues, were installed at the other hotels, until, as the minute says, there was not a hotel in all Orleans but was occupied, if not filled, by him or by the officers and men of his suite. His "college," that is, the ecclesiastics, twenty-five or thirty persons, were installed at the *Écu* (Crown) *de Saint Georges*; the choir and their leader at the *Enseigne de l'Épée* (Sign of the Sword); his armourer, Hector Broisset, at the *Coupe*; his brother, René de la Suze, at the *Petit Saumon* (Little Salmon); his councillors, Gilles de Sillé, Guy de Bonnière, Guyot de Chambrays, Guillaume Tardif, and Guy de Blanchfort, with his captain of the guard, Loys l'Angevin, at the *Grand Saumon* (Great Salmon); his chevaliers, Monseigneurs de Martigné, Foulques Blasmes, Jean de Rains, and Bauleis, at the *Image de Sainte Marie Madeleine*; Jean de Montecler, with Colin le Godelier; his *Rais le herault* (herald) and suite, with men-at-arms, at the *Tête Noire*; his chariots and horses, with those of his brother René, at the *Roche-Boulet*; the vicar of the chapel, the priest Le Blond and his barber, and the horses of the "college" at *l'Enseigne du Fourbisseur*; the Seignieur Jean de Veille, Bois-Roulier, his provost, George the trumpeter, at the house of Jeannette la Pionne; Thomas his *enlumineur*, at *le Dieu d'Amour* (God of Love); while men-at-arms, servants, lackeys, and followers, occupied the *Cheval Blanc* (White Horse), *l'Homme Sauvage* (Savage Man), and *l'Écu d'Orléans* (the Crown of Orleans).

While at Orleans, in 1434, he made thence, during the autumn, a trip to the Bourbonnais country, stopping for a time at Montlucon, at the hotel *l'Écu* (Crown) *de France*. When his hotel bill for eight hundred and ten *reaux d'or* was presented, he could pay only four hundred and ninety-five, and his two servitors, Jean de Sellier and Huet de Villarceau, became his guarantors of payment. Everything during the trip was at his expense. They all travelled on horseback, unless it was some high dignitary or *quelque malade* (sick) who had a chariot. Horses and all expenditures were furnished by him, and preparing for such a trip, everybody was provided with new, striking, and, consequently, expensive costumes, suitable for the suite of such a rich and puissant Baron.

On his return to Brittany in August, 1435, it was found that his travels during the year had cost the round sum of eighty thousand golden crowns. The *Mémoires* say this trip left a train of "devoured revenues, lands sold, seigniories mortgaged, works of art and valuables hypothecated, with considerable debts and unpaid loans *très onéreux*, which menaced ruin and opened an abyss threatening to engulf everything."

Among the records found at Orleans was one which, made under the circumstances relating to his expenses and financial condition, throws a strong side-light on his character, bringing out the recklessly spendthrift side of it, and would go a long way towards justifying the King's decree of the interdiction of the sale and mortgage of any property, which, it is not to be forgotten, shortly followed this visit to Orleans.

This paper, prepared by Gilles, provided:

"SATURDAY, XXVI DAY OF MARCH, MCCCCXXXIIII (1435 N.S.). The noble and puissant lord, Monsieur Gilles, Seignior of Retz, Count of Brienne, Lord of Champtocé and Pouzauges, Marshal of France, has lately, for the good of his soul, and looking to our Lord Jesus Christ, on behalf of himself, his late father, mother, relatives and friends, all sinners, made a foundation *in memory of the Holy Innocents*, at Machecoul in Rais, Duchy of Brittany."

By this paper he appoints a full corps of priests, "vicar, dean, archdeacon, treasurer, canons, chapter, and college"; for the support and maintenance of this establishment he gives in trust, in due and formal language, to the King of Sicily and Duke of Anjou his castle and *châtellenie* of Champtocé, and to the Duke of Brittany one-half the Barony and lands of Rais. He confirmed this gift before notaries named. He declared the two princes named should act as his trustees; and, providing for their possible refusal to act, he names respectively, and in succession, as future trustees, the King, the Emperor, the Pope; in case they all refuse, the lands shall be divided between the knights of the Orders of Saint John and of Saint Lazare.

All the Princes named refused, and each, as far as he could, interdicted and prohibited Gilles from carrying out his project. It accordingly fell through. Yet, at the moment of his establishing this priestly organisation, he was engaged, as we shall see farther on, in the commission of the most horrible and unnatural of crimes, for which he was, before the end of the decade, to be ignominiously executed.

His Maison de la Suze has been described, whether actually or only from similar houses of the epoch, is now impossible to tell; but it is said to have eclipsed, in its luxury and taste, the palace of the Dukes of Brittany. It was ornamented and decorated to a high degree. All countries were laid under tribute to furnish riches for its decoration: Italy for its painting and sculpture, Spain for its Cordovan leather, Flanders for its tapestry, Venice and Bohemia for their crystals and glassware, the Orient for its magnificent stuffs, and Persia for its tiles and *faience*; while, without doubt, the ceramics of his own and neighbouring provinces, like Tours, Orleans, Gien, Quimper, and Poitou (the latter the forerunner of Limoges), were represented in the luxurious fittings of the houses and châteaux of Gilles, the Baron de Retz.

The *Mémoire des Héritiers*, setting forth the extravagant and ruinous expenditures by which the principal of the estate was being dissipated, was duly presented to the King and the necessary proof offered to establish its allegations. The date is not given, but it should have been about 1432–33. In 1435–36, the King, having become satisfied of the truth of the matters alleged, through his Council of State and by letters patent, issued his decree of prohibition against the alienation or incumbrance by Gilles de Retz of any of his lands or seigniories. This decree has been preserved to us in Guepin's *Histoire de Nantes*, pp. 131–133.

The Decree of Interdiction by the King, against the sale and incumbrance of his property commences with a description of the various noble families from which Gilles de Retz had descended; his titles, his property, baronies, châteaux, seigniories, his marriage, the properties of his wife—that is to say, Pouzauges, Tiffauges, Chabenais, Confolens, Château-Morant, Savenay, Lombert, Grez-sur-Maine, and other beautiful properties, the rental value of which amounted to six or seven thousand livres (pounds, about three hundred thousand francs, actual value); that from his said marriage, he derived also personal property of the value of one hundred thousand golden crowns; that he held in Grosses Baronies thirty thousand livres of true domains; that from his office of Marshal of France he received grand salary and pension from the King, with numerous gratuities; so that he had a yearly income of forty or fifty thousand livres or more. The said Gilles, after the decease of his father, took the administration of his estate to himself and used it according to his pleasure; he established himself in an estate grander than that to which he really belonged; kept two hundred horsemen, maintained a chapel of singers in his château numbering twenty-five or thirty persons, chaplain, clerks, children, and others; these were taken with him when he travelled; and in all things he managed his affairs so as to have in his château, because of the said chapel, more than fifty men or persons at his expense, and as many horses; he had also in said chapel a great quantity or number of ornaments, cloth of gold, silk, chandeliers and *censoirs*, crosses, plates, dishes, etc.; these were of such sumptuosity that they cost three times more than their value; he had several organs, one of which, carried by six men, was taken with him wherever he went; he often purchased cloth-of-gold at sixty or eighty crowns per *aune* (ell) when it was not worth more than twenty-five, and a pair of "orfrays" (embroidered cloth of gold) at three or four hundred crowns, when they were not worth more than one hundred; he kept in the said chapel a dean, choir-leader, or singing-master, an archdeacon, vicar, schoolmaster, etc., as in the cathedral, and one of these priests or officers he undertook to establish and treat as a bishop; he paid to some of these four hundred crowns, and to others three hundred; he dressed them in robes with scarlet trains trimmed with plush and fur, with fine hats; all were kept and served with the most costly and expensive viands; the service of all these so-called priests (holy men) was nothing but vanity, without devotion and in defiance of good order. The said Gilles sent on several occasions to the Pope in the endeavour to obtain permission or authority that his choristers, or leaders, should be mitred as prelates, or like the canons of the church at Lyons. He made excessive gifts in wine, viands, and *hypocras*, to all who desired to eat or drink, keeping open house for that purpose, and those who had the government of his affairs lived like great lords; while the commoners frequently had naught, *ni boire ni manger*, when they came to table.

He played games, farces, *morisques*, and, on occasion, he performed the Mysteries of Pentecost and Ascension, on high scaffolds under which were *hypocras* and strong wines, as in a cave.

The said Gilles constituted one of his familiars, Roger de Briqueville, as his procureur, agent, or attorney-in-fact, empowered to marry his daughter, Marie, at a time when she was only four or five years of age, to whatever man should seem good to the said de Briqueville, against the custom prevailing in the country to marry the daughters, issue of such high nobility, only with the assent of their parents and friends. He took it into his head to deal in alchemy, hoping thus to obtain the Philosopher's Stone; sent to Germany and to different countries in search of the masters of this art, and brought to his château Monsieur Anth. of Palermo, making, with him, outrageous expenses from which no one derived any profit; in all of which things he acted without sense or understanding, and in a foolish, if not crazy, manner. It is found that he sold and alienated certain lands (describing them).

For these reasons, the King, being fully informed and having fully ascertained of the evil government of the said Sieur de Retz, through his Grand Council, issued his interdiction and prohibition against any alienation, transfer, mortgage, or pledge, by the said Gilles de Retz, of any of his lands or seigniories.

The King enjoined upon his Parliament the duty of carrying this decree of interdiction into effect; and under severe penalties, he forbade any captains, guards, tenants, or persons in charge, from attorning or delivering up to any stranger (to the title) any château or fortress of Gilles de Retz until Parliament should so order.

This decree was published "at the sound of the trumpet" at the principal places concerned—Orleans, Tours, Angers, Champtocé, Pouzauges, Tiffauges, Saint-Jean-d'Angely, and other places. The Duke of Brittany refused to accept, register, or publish the decree, and it was in vain that the "*femme, parents, et les amis*" of Gilles solicited him. It is alleged that this was to enable the Duke to take advantage of the necessities of Gilles, and purchase his lands at ruinous prices. He purchased some and took mortgages on others; Champtocé, Bourgneuf, Bénate, and Prinçay or Princé, were mortgaged for the sum of 100,000 crowns of gold, to be repaid within six years. In this way did Gilles, during these eight years of his life, dissipate the sum of *deux cents mille écus* (200,000 crowns) of the heritage.

The King's interdiction of the sale or mortgage of any of his property aggravated Gilles's situation by increasing his difficulties in obtaining money. He had no scruples about borrowing money of whomsoever he could, and if repayment could be put off a sufficient length of time, would promise the return of it doubled or trebled, as the creditor demanded. The situation must have been irritating to Gilles, and doubtless proved his incentive to magic, by which he hoped to discover the Philosopher's Stone, and, thereby, the means of converting the baser metals into gold. Whatever he may have done, or thought, in this direction prior to the passing of the decree, it seems that later he entered into closer relation with the alchemist and magician, and sought to study and practise the "black art" to a greater degree than he ever had done before.

From this on, we have to treat Gilles as a changed man, not only in his conduct, but in his character and desires. He separated from his wife, but established her in the château of Champtocé, while he installed himself with his retinue, including his magician, in the two châteaux, one at Machecoul, which he had received from his father, Guy de Laval, but principally at Tiffauges, which he had received from his wife. Here we have to treat of him no longer as a soldier, or as a noble of France, but in his character of magician, necromancer, debtor, robber, murderer.

Under these circumstances what course was Gilles to pursue,

and what could he do to retrieve his fallen fortunes? He required money, he was spending more than his income; he was selling off his property and reducing his principal in the vain attempt to liquidate his debts and provide for his present expenses. He did not have strength of character to adopt a rigorous reduction of expenses and live on a moderate and conservative plan; indeed, such would hardly have been natural. The great man of a neighbourhood, who, having been entrusted with large sums of money; or the banker or trader who, being deeply indebted, endeavours to restore his broken fortunes by retrenchment of expenditures, only precipitates the catastrophe he seeks to avert. The ostensibly rich man who proposes to make himself better able to meet the demands of his business by disposing of his horses and carriage, closing up his houses, selling his yacht, giving fewer entertainments to his friends, instead of proving himself successful and inviting confidence in his ability to pull through, will prove the architect of his own doom. Therefore, what was Gilles de Retz to do? What he did, was to rely upon the success of his scheme for the discovery of the Philosopher's Stone, in the hope to thus replenish his empty coffers.

CHAPTER IV

GILLES'S CRIMES

BEGINNING in the year 1432, a district comprising a large portion of western France, including the southern part of the Province of Brittany, the western part of the Province of Maine, and the northern part of the Province of Poitou, became excited by an undefined fear which, increased by its uncertainty and vagueness, produced in the people a feeling akin to terror. It was not the fear of war, for the people had had an intimate acquaintance with war for many years; nor was it the fear of an epidemic nor of sudden death; and it was not easy to tell with exactness what it was. It was so indefinite that belief in it was at first refused. It was considered by many to be the result of superstition; some declared it to be something of the vampire race which by some sort of resurrection had changed its horrible character so that it did not wait to prey upon the dead, but made its attacks upon the living, choosing young children and maidens, and timing the place and manner of attack so that not only was there no defence, but there was also no opportunity for pursuit or recovery.

Michelet (*Histoire de France*) describes it as a beast of extermination, unseen, unknown, unnatural, indescribable, invisible, supernatural, omnipresent, possessed of powers of disappearance on the instant, and so of escape, dissolving into thin air. It was believed by many to be a physical manifestation of the Evil One. It made its appearance in one place on one day and at another place the next day, and at a distant place the next; it was here to-night and far away in the morning; it ravaged the country, spreading terror, and leaving in its track not simply fear and mourning, but the torture of insanity and death. There was a mixture of enchantment, of impossibility, about the performance which left it to be accounted for only upon the principle of legerdemain, magic, the black art, and the presence of the devil. On all sides, right and left, east and west, north and south, within this terror-stricken district, sometimes each day for a week, sometimes not again for a month, then not for three, and again not for six months or more, but subject to these intervals, came the story from one section to the other, of the disappearance, as though by enchantment, of a child or children of tender age. No apparent distinction of sex was made, but the subjects of attack were always young, say from six to sixteen years; old enough to go about the farm or from one farm to another, possibly from one village to another, when, without warning, apparently without cause, without the slightest evidence as to the means used, and without leaving the slightest trace of the tragedy, suddenly a child was gone. No one knew or could find in what direction it had gone, or how it had been taken. All that the terror-stricken parents and family knew was that their child was here to-day, and now he or she was not—it was playing about the door only a half-hour since; now it was gone, gone as completely as though swallowed by the earth.

No one knew where the blow would fall next; no one knew whether his family circle was to be invaded, his house stricken, his child taken. Every care and watchfulness was employed, consultations were had between the stricken parents, the officers of the law were consulted, and all that was known—apparently all that could be discovered—was that their children were here yesterday, engaged in their little plays or about their own little duties around the house or on the farm, and in a moment, though the most rigorous and extensive search was made, they were gone—gone absolutely, gone beyond possibility of recovery, gone in numbers, gone from every part of the district mentioned, and no sign or trace left of their fate. Fear, fright, terror, took possession of all, and this, mixed with sorrow and grief, broke many a heart, sent many a loving mother in insanity to the grave. The peasants who, by reason of their age and strength supposed themselves to be safe, walked lightly, as though afraid to put their feet upon the ground; spoke in low voices as if afraid to trust themselves in ordinary tones, and everything throughout the country was done with bated breath as if in the presence of the dead.

The peasants, superstitious at the best of times, were now overcome with fear and gave themselves up a prey to the idea of enchantment and magic, and could only account for the disappearance of their loved ones by the presence of the arch-enemy of mankind, against whom they had no means of fighting, and whose assaults upon their devoted children they had no means of resisting. The frightened parents were tortured by the uncertainty of the fate that had overcome their loved ones. "Are they dead?" "Have they been taken to the realms above or to the tortures below?" "Are they in prison?" "Are they still living?" "Are they never to be seen again?" "Might they not be in a distant part of the country enduring pains and tortures?" "Might they not, even now, be weeping and screaming themselves half mad and demanding the presence and comfort of their mother?" "In what direction should we go?" "Has nobody seen them?" "Has search been made?" "In what direction have we yet to go?" No answer came to all these questions. The fate of the children was an impenetrable mystery.

Did the parents recover from it? Yes, they became accustomed to it. Human nature can become accustomed to anything. Their fate seemed better, not because it was better, but because, not getting worse, they got used to it and were able to stand it better. The first theory upon which the people settled was that the disappearance of their children was due to fairies, to evil genii, to a supernatural and mysterious enemy—that this mysterious enemy was supernatural, they did not doubt. This belief served to increase the pangs of their grief and to render the unknown and undiscoverable fate of their beloved ones more horrible to contemplate and more difficult for the parents to bear. They felt themselves incapable and incompetent to war against this mysterious, devastating, supernatural force; hence they resigned themselves to the affliction, considering it to have been sent upon them by Almighty God as a punishment for their sins. They did not know what sins they had committed, but felt sure that nothing they had done would justify even Almighty God in the abduction of the little ones who had not been at fault, and the torture of the parents incident thereto; so they rebelled against their fate.

The disappearance of children did not at first create great excitement among the people; their disappearance was explained in a natural manner: some accident had happened to them, possibly they had fallen into one of the many rivers and were drowned; the lakes and rivers were plentiful, their waters deep, their currents swift, the banks steep. One child here in one province, another child there in a distant province—such a disappearance did not count for much and did not unduly or wonderfully excite the people; but when it came to spread over the entire country and, by the comparison and the overlapping of searches and the employment of officers, it was discovered that this beast of extermination, this great, powerful, mysterious, supernatural visitor or power, was making itself felt throughout the entire country, and that no house was safe, that no parent could say with certainty that his own child might not be taken next morning—then the country became excited, alarmed, and, finally, terror-stricken.

At last it became apparent that these ravages were confined to a given district, a circle of country approximately bounded by the present cities of Vannes, Rennes, Angers, La Rochelle, and so opening to the ocean. Of this circle, Nantes was approximately the centre. This condition continued, growing more acute year by year. Each year new families were stricken, and the terror became more widely spread.

A man of the character and ambitions of Gilles de Retz would naturally have about him a corps of men to assist in carrying out his nefarious courses. They would necessarily be without fear and without conscience, adepts in secrecy and deceit, with the instincts and abilities of detectives and ready to obey any behest of their master. Gilles had such a corps of lieutenants; most of them were Bretons as he was, thoroughly acquainted with the country, most of them lowly born, many of them illegitimate and strongly suspected to have had fathers of higher birth than their mothers. Gilles made choice of these familiars from among his retinue, selecting those best qualified to carry out his projects and to be his right hand in executing his plans.

The names of some of these have been preserved to us in the process against Gilles: Eustache Blanchet, Henriet Griart, Jean Roussignol, Gilles de Sillé, Hugues de Bremont, Étienne Corrillaut (*alias* Poitou), Robin Romulart, and one woman, Perrine Martin, *alias* La Meffraye. These performed for Gilles the rôle of secretary, aide-de-camp, assistants, guards, spies, or servants, as occasion demanded, and became identified in the minds of the peasants as servants and representatives of Gilles de Retz. They spent practically their lifetime in his service, and toward the end of their career they came to be feared throughout the countryside as much as Gilles himself. Indeed, it was their actions which first attracted public attention towards him. It came to be noted that when infant or child had disappeared, some of these had been seen in the neighbourhood; and when all things pertaining thereto were so mysterious, the people stood ready to catch at any straw which might serve as a possible solution. The wiser persons, who were not so superstitious and did not attribute this disappearance of children to supernatural causes, but rather to the action of fiends, discovered and remarked the coincidence of the presence of some one of these with the disappearance of an infant. The attention of the officers was turned in his direction, and certain suggestions or suspicions were given to the Bishop of Nantes, who thereupon determined to open a secret inquest for the solution of the mystery. By this means the matter was brought to light.

The most prominent and powerful of these familiars of Gilles de Retz was an Italian priest and alchemist, François Prelati. He occupied a position different from the others. One of the before-mentioned familiars, Eustache Blanchet, a *soi-disant* priest, belonging to his ecclesiastical retinue, appears to have been better acquainted with the private affairs of Gilles de Retz than any other, and to have been entrusted with higher powers, and sent oftener on journeys of diplomacy and confidential business. For what purpose he should have been sent to Italy can now only be surmised; but in the year 1436, while in Florence, he met François Prelati. His history has been given by Saunière, but no one knows how much of it is fact and how much is romance. It appears, however, that Prelati was born in Mont Catane in the Valle Nero; that he was educated as an ecclesiastic, admitted to orders, and given the tonsure by the Bishop of Arezzo. He became interested in the study of the occult sciences, especially chemistry or, as it was then called, alchemy; and his love for this science overcame his desire for ecclesiastical service.

He was about forty-five years of age when he became acquainted with Gilles de Retz; was well bred, highly educated, of elegant manners, handsome in appearance, well kept and cleanly in person, devoting much care to the welfare of his hair, beard, and hands, all of which repaid and showed the attention bestowed upon them. He was a good conversationalist, of smooth, insinuating, and seductive manner. He spoke Latin as well as he did Italian; his French was excellent, probably better than that of Gilles or the Bretons with whom he associated, while a slightly broken pronunciation conspired to make it more attractive. He had a brilliant and sparkling wit and an active imagination, was well posted in the affairs of the world, and attractive to his fellows, whether men of letters, men of affairs, or *des hommes de guerre*. The description given of him would indicate his appearance to have been that of an elegant gentleman. It goes without saying that he was learned as an alchemist and expert as a necromancer. Such was François Prelati, the man who had been brought by Eustache Blanchet from Italy to France to teach Gilles de Retz the black art.

Gilles, during this period, occupied alternately, according to his pleasure, the two châteaux of Machecoul and Tiffauges. The latter is situated to the north of the village of Tiffauges and, according to tradition, occupies the site of an ancient Roman camp and is about 15 kilometres south of Clisson and 40 south of Nantes. The château occupies an elevated plateau which forms a promontory between the junction of the creek Crume with the river Sèvre, both of which bathed the foot of the walls on either side. The latter continues its way northward and empties into the Loire below Nantes. The château was a castle covering space enough for a city. It is now in ruins, except the grand tower and adjacent halls. The walls may be traced by the débris in rows of stones now covered with sod and grass. It was attacked and burned during the religious wars of the sixteenth century, but its present ruinous condition began with the breaking-out of the Revolution in 1789. The Vendeans, after gaining the battle of Torfou, occupied it, having repaired it sufficiently to afford shelter and to make it a place of defence. It remained in a fairly good condition until the return of Napoleon from Elba, when it was again occupied as a recruiting-place, or place of security by the Vendeans. After the battle of Waterloo and the restoration of Louis XVIII., fearing some further use of it by enemies, the government destroyed it, reducing it to its present condition. The lowlands in the neighbourhood are marshy and almost become lakes. The lake of Grand Lieu is not far distant, and others are in the vicinity.

The ruins are interesting and the débris is easily recognised. One with a slight knowledge of the arrangement can trace the walls of the structure, as well as the triple cincture of fortifications surrounding it. These are now covered with sod and green grass and used for pasturage, while the level places, like the courts within the castle and the parade-ground within the lines of fortification, are subjected to cultivation. The château of Tiffauges was partially built in the time of Saint Louis; the grand tower now remaining is said to belong to that epoch; the large tower, the small tower, the chapel, the great hall wherein the Baron presided over his retainers or, if need be, received such lords and seigniors as came to visit him; the dining-room, kitchen, scullery, with all their necessary appurtenances of cellar, storehouse, warehouses, well-room, were all in evidence; bedrooms, halls, parlours, etc., were prepared in abundance for the reception of lords, ladies, and all who might attend upon the occasion of a ball or fête. On another side of the courtyard, but adjoining the main building, was a shorter wing, large enough to lodge his knights, men-at-arms, soldiers, servants, varlets, etc. It was, in these regards, similar to most other extensive castles or châteaux, and can be compared to the château of Nantes where Gilles was tried and convicted. (See frontispiece.)

The Château Tiffauges was a favourite residence of Gilles de Retz; it was a stronghold, in which, if need be, he could have great security and, in case of war or attack, could make a good defence. It was large and commodious. Here it was that Gilles de Retz and François Prelati, the Italian, had their laboratory in which they endeavoured, first by alchemy, then by magic, and lastly by murder, to discover the Elixir of Eternal Youth and the transmutation of metals into gold. Here took place the attempt to obtain a conference with the Evil One, with the idea of obtaining his supposed influence in their sublunary affairs.

A description of this laboratory has been left us. The chamber was high up in the tower, with communicating passages in various directions,—to the large tower and also to the basement and, as is said, to the *oubliettes* and the secret passageway to the Crume and so outside the château. The laboratory occupied the full diameter of the tower; an immense chimney was on one side of the room, in which was placed the furnace where the mutilated bodies of many of the dead infants were consumed.

The chamber had but two windows, one to the north the other to the south, both high up in the wall, both capable of being closed and darkened by solid shutters.

Lemire says (p. 27):

"In the highest chamber of the small tower, he [Gilles] had installed a chemical [alchemy] laboratory and there employed his three sorcerers, one French, one English or Picardian, and one Italian";

And he describes with minutest detail the apparatus employed (p. 28):

"What Gilles desired was that Prelati should make gold, whether by science, by magic, by the intervention of the devil, or by these means united. He attempted the transmutation of metals into gold. He distilled into retorts different liquids destined to dissolve the mineral substances after certain formulas of magic repeated under the invocation of demons. Prelati declared to Gilles that to make these operations successful required the addition of the hearts, hands, or eyes, but above all the blood, of young children. The blood was to be used in tracing the magic circles and figures."

Lemire believes (p. 30) that Prelati employed the secrets of chemical art, sulphur and phosphorus and similar substances, in forming fiery serpents to deceive Gilles:

"Frogs and serpents, inoffensive but frightful in appearance, a leopard which was naught else than a large dog with bristling hair, cries of beasts, groans, sounds of trumpets; these were the apparatus employed in the scenes of invocation."

Then he tells (p. 31) how, to furnish victims for these magicians, Gilles carried on his abduction of children, choosing the little peasants who would not be missed, or whose parents would not be likely, from poverty, to pursue the search.

Apparently the first step, at least the first step made public, against Gilles de Retz, charging him with crime, and the first paper forming part of the ecclesiastical record in the archives of the Department of Loire-Inférieure, is the "Declaration of Infamy against Gilles de Retz by the Bishop of Nantes, July 30, 1440." It was in Latin:

"To all to whom these present letters shall come, Jean, by the permission of the holy apostolic see, Bishop of Nantes, with full assurance of salvation through our Lord and Saviour, salute those present:

"We hereby make known by visiting in person the parish of the Holy Mary at Nantes, in which is built the house or château vulgarly called "la Suze," the frequent habitation of Gilles de Retz hereinafter described, a parishioner of this church and of other parish churches designated further on. Upon public rumour and on the numerous reports that have come upon us by the denunciatory clamour of Agatha, wife of Denis de la Mignon; of Donété, widow of the defunct Regnaud Donété of St. Marie; of Jean Guibert and his wife of St. Vincent; of the widow Eonnet Kerguen of St. Croix, Nantes; of Jeanne, wife of Jean Darell of St. Similien near Nantes; of Theophanie, wife of Eonnet le Charpentier of St. Clement outside the walls; fortified by the depositions of the synodical witnesses of these churches and by men who, thanks to their probity and their well known prudence, are above suspicion, and who, in the course of our pastoral visit in the same churches, we ourselves have interrogated with the greatest care upon the facts below indicated, or of still others pertaining to the duty of the bishop in his pastoral visits, we have discovered, and the depositions of the witnesses have proved to us, among other things, that Gilles de Retz, our subject and justiciable, by himself or by certain men his accomplices, has strangled, killed, and inhumanly massacred a very large number of infants; that he has committed upon them crimes against nature; that he has made, or has caused to be made, numerous horrible invocations of demons; he has made to them sacrifices and offerings, and has passed a compact with them, without counting other crimes, numerous and enormous, all of which belong within our jurisdiction; and, finally, by several other visits made by us or by the Commissary acting in our name, we know that Gilles de Retz has perpetrated and committed these crimes and still others, within the limits of our diocese.

"For which cause he was, and is now, and publicly for the knowledge of all, rendered infamous towards all grave and honest men. And to the end that no person shall have doubt upon this subject, we have ordained, or fixed, or caused to be fixed, our seal to these present letters.

"Given at Nantes, the day before the last of July, in the year of our Lord, 1440.

"By the command of Monseignior, Bishop of Nantes.

(*Signed*)
"J. Petit."

It does not appear that this declaration of infamy was ever made known to Gilles de Retz. It was made by the Bishop of Nantes in accordance with his ecclesiastical right and duty. It had, from early Christian times, been the duty of the bishops of the Church to make episcopal visits throughout their respective dioceses. By the capitularies of Charlemagne and Carloman, it became the bishop's right, if not his duty, to listen to any complaints of the common people. This was in the nature of an inquest by church authority into the crimes of high or powerful persons, or into public scandals which were without other rectification. The proceeding might be likened to an ecclesiastical grand jury. It was, like that of the grand jury, a secret inquest, *inquisitio famæ*, and in this particular instance, establishing the infamy of Gilles, it opened against him the inquisitory proceeding according to the rule: *Inquisitionem debet clamosa insinuatio prævenire.* This declaration of infamy, made by the bishop and based upon the complaints he had received and scandals he had heard during his episcopal visit, was the beginning of the prosecution against Gilles.

The secret investigation doubtless continued and culminated in the citation of the Bishop to Gilles de Retz, September 13th, to appear on September 19th, and answer the charges. After the preamble and declarations of the requisite power and authority, and his knowledge of the crimes of Gilles and of the public clamour, called in the official document *hurlements ululantium*, the bishop proceeds:

"For these causes we will no longer hide the monstrous things, nor will we allow heresy to develop itself, that heresy which, like a cancer, devours everything if it is not promptly extirpated even to the last root. Farther than that, we would apply a remedy as prompt as it is efficacious. Therefore we enjoin you, all and singular, and to those of you in particular to whom the present letter shall come, immediately and in a definite manner, each for himself and without counting on the other, without depending upon the care of any other, to cite before us, or before the official of our cathedral church, on Monday, the fête-day of the Exaltation of the True Cross, September 19, Gilles, as aforesaid designated the Baron of Retz, to submit to our authority and to accept our jurisdiction; we ourselves cite him by these letters to appear before our bar to respond to the crimes that are laid upon him. Execute, therefore, these orders, you, and each of you, and every one of you, cause them to be executed.

"Given at Nantes on Tuesday, the 13th of September, in the year of our Lord, 1440.

"By the command of the Bishop of Nantes.

(*Signed*)
"JEAN GUIOLE."

Whether the Bishop of Nantes had, in his official capacity, already established a permanent ecclesiastical court for the trial of such cases as might properly be brought before it, does not appear; nor whether he had the necessary paraphernalia of officers such as prosecutors, clerks, record-keepers, and an executive officer to serve processes, maintain order, etc., etc., as would be usual and necessary in all regularly established courts. So it is not known whether the executive officer charged with the service of this writ was a regular officer, or only one appointed for the occasion; but it abundantly appears that one Robert Guillaumet, a notary of Nantes, received the writ for execution, and that in this matter he acted as executive officer for the Bishop.

Gilles de Retz was at that time at his château of Machecoul. Robert Guillaumet took to his aid Jean l'Abbé, a captain in the service of the Duke of Brittany, with a number of his troop, and together they repaired to Machecoul for the purpose of arresting Gilles on the warrant of the Bishop.

There has been some discussion over the part taken in the affair by the Duke of Brittany himself, and how far the proceeding met his approval, and how far he stood ready to give aid and assistance in carrying out the purpose of the Bishop. Michelet (*Histoire de France*, vol. v.) asserts that the Duke of Brittany was highly favourable to the accusation; that "he was delighted at the opportunity to thus strike at a Laval," and he ascribes this to the fact that the Laval family, though related to the Montforts, of which the Duke was one, had formed against him an opposition, the intention of which was to deliver Brittany to France. There can be but little doubt that the Duke of Brittany was entirely favourable to the Bishop—they were near relatives and good friends, they always had stood together, and though the Bishop never had had any dispute with Gilles de Retz, yet the Duke frequently had.

The Duke had already foreseen the waning fortune of Gilles, and stood ready to profit by it. He had refused to make publication in Brittany of the decree of interdiction of the King, for the sake of the opportunity which might accrue to obtain good bargains in purchasing the property of Gilles. It is scarcely possible, dependent as he must have been upon the Duke and his government and the power and force of the secular arm for the execution of any decree that might be passed, that the Bishop of Nantes would proceed against so powerful a baron as Gilles, the dean of the nobility of Brittany, Marshal of France, and Lieutenant-General of the Duke's army, and enter upon an undertaking so gigantic, so fraught with danger, and so easy to miscarry, without having first consulted with, and obtained the approval and favour of, his sovereign, with the promise of material assistance and governmental aid in case of need. This understanding between the Bishop and the Duke is established by the outcome of the process. We see that in every step the Bishop not only received countenance and favour at the hands of the Duke, but that he could be relied upon to furnish the necessary strong arm for the execution of the Bishop's writs and decrees.

Armed with the writ and warrant of arrest, Robert Guillaumet and Jean l'Abbé proceeded to Machecoul with their troop of soldiers. What was their reception? Would they be successful in their undertaking and bring the mighty Baron of Retz back to Nantes as prisoner? Would he yield to the mandates of the law, obey the command of the Bishop, and surrender himself as prisoner? He had a château, a veritable stronghold, and he had his army of retainers within it—he could defy both Robert Guillaumet with his writ and Jean l'Abbé with his escort—but would he do so? Would he resist or would he yield? Michelet passes the highest encomiums upon this little band, whose intrepidity and courage he lauds as though it was leading a forlorn hope, for its devotion to duty in entering upon so dangerous a procedure as this arrest. There does not seem, however, to have been any reasonable apprehension of danger. If Gilles resisted arrest, he would simply remain within his castle, refuse to open his gate, and bid defiance to the officers. They would then return to Nantes and report their failure, and what would be done further was a matter for their superiors, the authorities of the kingdom.

There may have been speculations as to what moved Gilles to surrender, and no one can tell with certainty what thus influenced him. He had three alternatives: resist arrest and fight it out with the authorities, drive back the officers and then flee the country, or submit to arrest. To shut himself up in his castle and resist arrest would bring down the entire power of the kingdom, he would be excommunicated by the Church and besieged by the Duke's army—there was little prospect of success in that direction. Flight would be a confession of guilt, while he would have to leave everything behind—it would be practically impossible for him to take his fortune or even any considerable amount of valuables with him, and he would soon become poverty-stricken and an outcast. It is more likely that he pursued the conservative course of submitting to arrest, trusting to his rank, fortune, power, and the law's failure to make proof against him, hoping by these to evade conviction.

That he was technically guilty of both heresy and sacrilege there could be but little doubt, and it appears that he had greater fear of these charges than of the others. When he found these were not to be pressed, and that he was to be charged with the abduction of infants, he may have felt stronger in the knowledge that he had never personally committed these crimes, and that they could not be directly proved against him. It is to be remembered that these offences had been running for eight years; that they had been committed in all parts of the country, always in isolated places, east, west, north, south; and Gilles may have come to the conclusion, during the long series of years, that whatever might be proved against his accomplices and active agents, nothing could ever be proved against him. And now, as he must make a decision immediately upon the arrival of Robert Guillaumet with his warrant, Gilles may have felt that the shortest and easiest way was the best. Partly, then, from pride, from policy, from bravado, and in the belief that he would be able to defeat his adversaries in their proofs, he gave orders to lower the bridge, to raise the portcullis, and to open the gates of the castle.

Submitting himself to arrest, he is reported to have said: "I have always had the design to become a monk, and here comes the Abbé to whom I now engage myself" (*Procès Célèbres*: Paris, 1858, p. 14). Robert Guillaumet and Jean l'Abbé made search of the castle. Prelati, Poitou, and Henriet were arrested with Gilles at the château; Blanchet was taken in the town; but most of the retinue of Gilles escaped. Then the escort of Jean l'Abbé put themselves in order of march, guarding their prisoners. Arrived at the château of Nantes, the gates were opened, and Gilles de Retz, the dean of the barons of Brittany, Marshal of France, and his party, were conducted within its heavy walls as prisoners and malefactors. Gilles was assigned one of the upper chambers in the *Tour Neuve* of the château, and here he remained during the trial, until the last day, when he was probably placed in the condemned cell. His accomplices were not treated with the same consideration, but were thrown pell-mell into the common prison of the castle.

The château of Nantes (frontispiece) is really a castle and would be called such in England or in English-speaking countries. It was built by, and had always belonged to, the government, first to the Duke and afterward to the King. Its construction dates from the tenth century. It was commenced by Conan, a Count of Rennes, an usurper, who commenced the castle as a stronghold, by the possession of which he hoped to resist the lawful claimant of the duchy and overawe the inhabitants of the city. That portion called *Tour Neuve* was built at this epoch, situated at the confluence of the river Eure with the Loire, and the waters of each of these rivers originally bathed the foot of the walls. Conan did not long enjoy his possessions in Nantes; he was attacked and overthrown, and Americ de

Thouars took possession under the title of Count of Nantes. During this epoch was built the château of Champtoceau, which figured as the place of the capture of Clisson.

In the year 1207, Guy de Thouars repaired the château of Nantes, and in 1227, Pierre de Dreux enlarged it, and so it remained until the time of Francis II., when, under Du Cherfan in 1480 to 1499, it was enlarged to its present dimensions. The bastion or *Tour Mercœur*, constructed in 1588 by the duke of that name, then Governor of Nantes, was situated at the angle of State Street and Port Maillaird. It has been renewed and restored sundry times since then, but not to affect the integrity of the building as a whole. The *Tour Neuve* was the prison of Gilles de Retz, and in the second story was the grand hall or audience-chamber in which the ecclesiastical court was held.

The château of Nantes has figured largely in the history of Brittany and France. It was the official residence of the Count of Nantes. The Duke of Brittany resided there when in the city. So also it was occupied by the kings of France and other great and noble personages during their passage through, or temporary residence in, the city. Charles VIII. and Duchess Anne were married in its chapel. The celebrated Edict of Nantes, issued by Henry IV., King of France, in April, 1598, by which the Protestants were permitted to exercise their religion without hindrance, was passed and signed in this building. In 1654, the Cardinal of Retz (not to be confounded with Gilles de Retz) was a prisoner here, and thence made his escape. Minister Fouché was prisoner in this château; Madam Sévigné was also held here in 1648; in 1842, the Duchess of Berry was also prisoner in this château.

CHAPTER V

GILLES'S TRIAL BEFORE THE
ECCLESIASTICAL TRIBUNAL

THE ecclesiastical trial Against Gilles de Retz was of course conducted by the Bishop. He was the representative of the Church in the diocese, and he alone had the authority to act. His name was Jean de Malestroit. He was originally Bishop at St. Brieuc, but had been Bishop of Nantes since 1419. He called, as his assistants in the trial, to aid by their counsel and advice, the Bishops of Mans, of St. Brieuc, and of Saint Lo, one of the officials of the Church at Nantes, and with them Pierre de l'Hospital, President of the High Court of Brittany, and whose aid was asked to represent the civil law and to direct the charges, the witnesses, and the debates in such manner that they should come within the civil law. Three of the notaries of Nantes were made clerks, with a foreign assistant. Robert Guillaumet was the executive officer, that is to say, the sheriff or bailiff of the court. The prosecuting officer appointed by the Bishop was William Chapeillon, the Curé of St. Nicholas at Nantes.

It has been said that the Bishop, for a considerable length of time, had been receiving and hearing complaints and charges against Gilles de Retz, and that especially during the last month he had been investigating their truth. In this he was aided by the aforesaid William Chapeillon, who would thus have been entirely familiar with the charges against Gilles de Retz. It was, therefore, eminently proper that he should be appointed prosecutor. Whether the Bishop had the full power under either the civil law or the ecclesiastical law, to make the foregoing appointments of colleagues on his own motion and according to his own will, is not here determined, nor does it appear, in making these appointments, whether the accused was consulted or whether he gave his consent, nor does it appear that he either took or had the right to take exception to them or any of them and by such exception deprive them of the right to act in his case. As to one aid to the Bishop, Gilles's consent was asked and obtained before he was allowed to sit, that was Brother Jean Blouyn, of the Order of *Frères-Prêcheurs* at the Convent at Nantes. He had been appointed as Vice-Inquisitor for the diocese of Nantes by the authority of the Grand Inquisitor of France, B. N. Medici, who had been appointed to that office by the Pope. Great stress is laid, throughout the process wherever this appointment came in question, on the fact that Gilles de Retz had consented to it before the priest took his seat on the bench. Jean Blouyn was a man of about forty years of age, who seemed to have commended himself for his moderation in making a decision, and for his firmness in adhering to it. Abbé Boussard classes him as *digne de tout éloge et apprécié de tout le monde.*

Another tribunal represented the civil law, and it was by this that the secular sentence of execution was passed.

In France, as in all countries under the civil or Roman law, and in some of the countries under the common law, there has been a separate jurisdiction of certain offences for the ecclesiastical court. As a matter of course, and necessary for the continuance and good administration of justice, there would be some controversies of which these two courts would have concurrent jurisdiction. It is quite impossible in such a work as the present to go into this question. Those who are interested in the subject are respectfully referred, for France, to the *Histoire du droit criminel en France* (pp. 74 and 85) by Du Boys; to Faustin-Helie's *Traité de l'instruction criminelle*; Fornier's *Les officialités au moyen âge*; Esmien's *Histoire de la procédure criminelle en France, et spécialment de la procédure inquisitoriale depuis le XIIIme siècle jusqu'à nos jours* (Paris, 1882); and for the general criminal procedure and jurisdiction of the ecclesiastical tribunal, to Beiner's *Beitrage zu der Geschichte der Inquisition, prozesses* (pp. 16–78). For a general history of these subjects as applied to England, one should consult the great work on the *History of Common Law*, by Sir Henry Maine.

The record of the process against Gilles de Retz in the archives of the Department of Loire-Inférieure has been adverted to. We now come to a point where it is almost the entire evidence. It consists of the records of the two courts, one the ecclesiastical court, kept by the clerks before-mentioned, and to which the names of some one or all of three are signed for each day, either Jean Delaunay, Jean Petit, Guillaume Lesne, or Nicholas Giraud. This record, made each day, apparently was supervised and made official by the prosecutor, William Chapeillon, and it seems that more than one copy was made of it at that time. This was in Latin, though French was interjected occasionally. The other record was of the civil tribunal, the record of the day's proceedings being reduced to writing and signed by Touscheronde as Commissioner of the civil court, or by one of his aids, or, as they call them, *assesseurs*, who signed, alternating with Touscheronde. Their names were, Nicholas Chatau, Michael Eveillard, and Jean Coppegorge. This record was kept in French, the vulgar tongue, and very bad French and a very vulgar tongue it was. It would be interesting to philologists to note the changes during the last five hundred and fifty years in the spelling and, doubtless, pronunciation of the words of the French language.

These two records of the trial, the ecclesiastical and the civil, are treated as one, and their originals are filed together in the archives of the Department of Loire-Inférieure in the locality designated as Coté E, 189. Four copies of this record have been made, two in the year 1530, one of which was at the request of Gilles de Laval, the other for the Sire de la Tremoille. The copy given to the family of Laval has disappeared and no trace of it is known; the other for Tremoille was placed in the château of

Thouars which, it is to be remembered, was the family name of the wife of Gilles de Retz.

This copy has taken its name from this château and is known in history as the Manuscrit de Thouars. It was left in this château until its existence was forgotten. When the château was bought by the State and became part of the national domain, all papers and documents belonging to the family were transported to the château of Serrant in Anjou, of which one of the ladies of the family of Tremoille was mistress. This copy of the record was in a pile of documents, tossed pell-mell and without order, and here Monsieur Marchegay, the archivist of the Department of Maine-et-Loire, discovered it. The Duke de la Tremoille immediately took steps for its preservation. This record was on parchment like the original, and comprises four hundred and twenty pages, of which three hundred and three, in Latin, are the record of the ecclesiastical trial; the last hundred and eight pages constitute the record of the civil tribunal, and are in French.

Two other copies have been made in modern times, one for the Bibliothèque Nationale, Paris, made under the Second Empire, and one for the Public Library at Carpentras, both of which have been certified as true. The author procured a photograph of an open page from the original ecclesiastical record in the archives at Nantes. It was made on his personal application while he was Consul of the United States at Nantes. These records will be explained in this work, and upon their foundation rests the entire history of Gilles de Retz. Without this record or its copies, the true story of Bluebeard could not be written.

Michelet (*Histoire de France*, vol. v., pp. 208 *et seq.*), in his description of the arrest and trial of Gilles de Retz, depends on two manuscript copies which he mentions in a note; one in the Bibliothèque Royale (No. 493 F)—the other communicated to him by M. Louis Du Bois.

The warrant of arrest of Gilles de Retz was signed by the Bishop on the 13th of September, 1440, it was executed the next day, the 14th, and on that day Gilles was thrown in prison.

On the 19th, five days after, he was brought before the Bishop in the great hall of the *Tour Neuve*, in the château of Nantes. No information had been prepared, and no indictment filed. The prosecutor informed Gilles that he was charged with the crime of heresy and asked if he was willing to be tried before the ecclesiastical court, to which he consented, and added, with a defiant air full of assurance, that he would recognise in advance any other ecclesiastical judges, as he had great desire to clear himself of such accusation in the presence of any inquisitor, *n' importe lequel*. It was on this occasion that the Bishop of Nantes called to his aid as an auxiliary judge, Jean Blouyn of the Order of *Frères-Prêcheurs*, the Vice-Inquisitor of the faith for the diocese of Nantes, and then, this business having been brought to a close, the session of the court was adjourned until the 28th of September, when the witnesses would be heard.

The record of this session is rendered in Latin, a translation of which is here given: (Translation)[3]

"*Monday, September* 19, 1440.

"Proces-verbal, appearance in court of
Gilles de Retz and his submission to the
jurisdiction of the Court.

"On aforesaid Monday after aforesaid feast of the Exaltation of the Holy Cross, there appeared personally in court before the afore-mentioned reverend Father the Lord Bishop of Nantes, in the great hall of the new tower of the castle of Nantes, to give hearing before the tribunal holding session there, the honourable Guillermus Chapiellon, promoter of cases of office of the aforesaid court, reproducing in fact the letters of citation enclosed above, together with the enclosed execution of them,—

---

3   The entire ecclesiastical record was written in Latin with an occasional interjection of French.

78

there appeared this Chapeillon on the one hand, and on the other the aforesaid M. Egidius, soldier and baron, the accused. And this M. Egidius [Gilles], soldier and baron, after he in his wisdom had perceived that the promoter accused him of heresy, said that he wished to appear before the aforesaid reverend Father the Lord Bishop of Nantes, and some other ecclesiastical judges, also before the inquisitor for heretical wickedness, and to purge himself of the crimes laid against him. Then the aforesaid reverend Father appointed for the aforesaid Monsieur soldier and baron, who agreed in this, the 28th day of the aforesaid month to legitimately appear before the religious, the brother Jean Blouyn, the vicar of the inquisitor of cases of heretical wickedness, in the afor-mentioned place, to answer to the crimes and charges to be urged against him by the aforesaid promoter, . . . to be tried in things pertaining to faith, as is lawful and proper . . .

"In the presence of the distinguished men Master Oliverio Solidi de Beauveron, and M. Johannis Durandi of Blain, rector of the parochial churches, of the diocese of Nantes, called as witness to the foregoing."

The commission of Jean Blouyn as Vice-Inquisitor was written in Latin on parchment, to which was attached the great seal in red wax, which hung dangling by two silken cords. It was as follows:

"William Merici, of the order of Friars Preachers, professor of Sacred Theology, by the apostolic authority Grand Inquisitor of Heresy in the Kingdom of France, to our well-beloved brother in Jesus Christ, Jean Blouyn of the convent of our order in the city of Nantes, salvation by the author of our faith, the Lord Jesus Christ:

"Heresy, says the Apostle, is an evil that, if not cut up by the roots by the iron of the Inquisition, will propagate itself as a cancer in secret, and in darkness bring death to the most simple soul. Thus, in order to proceed in the interest of their own salvation against heretics, their aiders and abettors, and the evil men, because of heresy or suspected of the crime, against those who oppose the Inquisition, or who restrict its free agency, it is necessary to proceed with great caution and rare prudence. We have fullest confidence in the Lord that you are endowed with a capacity, jurisdiction, and good will to exercise this high charge. For this reason, by the counsel of several of our brothers of which the wisdom is recognised by all, we have made, established, and created to-day, and by these presents we do make, establish, and create you in all forms and with all the conditions required by the law and the best authority which are in our hands, as our vicar in the city and diocese of Nantes.

"By these letters, then, and by this concession, power is given to you against heretics and against the culpable persons above designated which may be there or otherwise. Also requests, citations, interviews, interrogations, you can take against all; you can cause them to be retained prisoners and proceed against them in justice in any manner that you may judge convenient, even including a definite sentence. You will have finally all that by custom or by law belong to the charge of Inquisitors; for in all this, as well as by the force of the common law as by the grace of spiritual privileges enjoyed by the Inquisition, we give to you, as much as it is in all our power.

"In testimony of which, we have set our hand and seal to these letters patent.

(*Signed*)
"G. MERICI.

"Done at Nantes *July* 25, 1426."

This letter was read to Gilles, and he was asked if he recognised it. He declared "No!" It was submitted to, and proved by, the court, and was recognised as authentic and genuine, and under its authority Brother Jean Blouyn was admitted to a seat upon the bench as representative of the Holy Inquisition and as judge in the case, aid to the Bishop.

The session of October 11th was ended, and Gilles led back to prison.

On Wednesday the judges met, not in the great audience chamber, but in the hall below, *aula bassa.* It was, and is, the custom in the prosecution of criminal cases to have the investigation of the witnesses before either the court or some high officer of justice prior to the public or official trial. In this investigation the procedure corresponds in some degree to that of our grand jury, or more properly before the prosecuting attorney as well as the presiding judge. The inquests made by the Bishop of Nantes, and with him his present prosecuting attorney, William Chapeillon, during the summer preceding, had been secret, the witnesses having been called up separately and examined privately; but on this occasion the session was open, at least to all witnesses, and, as Michelet describes them,

"a cloud of witnesses, poor people, came up single file, crying and sobbing while they recounted the details of the abduction of their children. Their cries and tears added to the horror of the crimes which they recounted and showed the great sorrow and grief to which they had been subjected, and the terrors through which they had passed."

The following is a record of this session, and the depositions of the witnesses heard:

"*Wednesday, September* 28, 1440.

"Procès-verbal de réception des plaintes.

"The register in the case and cases of faith, in the presence of the Reverend Father in Christ, lord Jean de Malestroit, Bishop of Nantes, and of brother Jean Blouyn, vicar of Father Guillermus Merici, the inquisitor mentioned below, against M. Egidius (Gilles) de Rays, soldier, lord, and baron of the same place, under accusation.

"In the name of the Lord, Amen.

"In the year of the Lord 1440, on Wednesday, September 28, in the third indiction, in the tenth year of the pontificate of our most holy Father in Christ and Lord Eugenius IV., Pope by divine providence, and during the session of the council of Basle, there appeared before . . . the lord bishop Johannes de Malestroit, . . . and brother Johannes de Blouyn, . . . vicar of Guillermus Merici, the inquisitor in matters of heretical wickedness, . . . and before their scribes, . . . the persons to be mentioned below, who, . . . in tears and sorrows complained of the loss of their children and grandchildren and of others mentioned below, asserting that these children and others had, by the aforesaid Egidius de Rays and certain other accomplices of his and his abettors, been treacherously carried off and inhumanly strangled, and that he had committed upon them sins against nature, . . . that he had often invoked evil spirits and offered homage to them, and had committed very many other enormous and unheard-of crimes of which the ecclesiastical court takes cognizance . . .

"Of whom the first complainant is Agatha the wife of Denys de la Mignon, of the parish of Holy Mary of Nantes, stating that a certain Colin her grandchild, the son of Guillermus Apvrill, about 20 years of age, small of stature and white of face, having on one ear a birth-mark, in the year 1439 in the month of August or thereabouts, on a Monday morning early went to the house commonly called la Suze in the city of Nantes (belonging to and occupied by Baron de Rays) . . . And afterwards she did not see the aforesaid Colin nor did she hear anything about him until a certain Perrina Martini *alias la Meffraye*, was arrested and shut up in the prisons of the secular court of Nantes. After this arrest she says that she heard it said by many that very many boys and innocent children had been carried off and killed by M. de Rays, she does not know to what purpose.

"Likewise the widow of Reginald Donété of the parish of Holy Mary of Nantes, also complained that Jean her son and son of aforesaid Donété used to frequent the house de la Suze in the city of Nantes; and since the feast of St. John the Baptist of the year 1438 she heard nothing about him until the aforesaid Perrina Martin, *alias la Meffraye*, was arrested and imprisoned and confessed that she had given him over to the aforesaid de Rays and his companions.

"Johanna, the wife of Guibeleti Delit, of the Parish of St. Denys of Nantes, likewise complained that her son Guillermus used to visit the house de la Suze, and went there during the first week of last Lent; and she had heard M. Jean Briant say that he had seen him in the aforesaid house on seven or eight successive days; that she had never afterwards seen her son, and that she suspected that he had been put to death in that house.

"Johannes Hubert and his wife, parishioners of St. Vincent of Nantes, complained that a certain son of theirs Jean by name, about 14 years of age, went to the house la Suze two years before the feast of the Nativity of St. John of last year, and then returning to the house of his parents, told his mother that he had cleansed the room of the aforesaid de Rays in the house de la Suze and had therefor bread in the aforesaid house, which bread he brought home and gave to his mother; to whom he also said that he was in favour with M. de Rays, and that the lord had given him white wine to drink; consequently he immediately returned to the house of Suze and was never again seen by his parents.

"Johanna, the wife of Johannes Darel, of the parish of St. Similien near Nantes, complained that on the feast of Sts. Peter and Paul of the year before last, she was going home from the church of Nantes in the evening, and a child of hers aged seven or eight years was following her. When she had reached the church of St. Saturnine of Nantes, or was near it, she looked around to see her son, whom she thought to be following her, but she saw him neither then nor ever after.

"The wife of Yvon Kyeguen, stonecutter, of the parish of the Holy Cross of Nantes, complained that she had given to a certain Poitou, a servant of M. de Rays, one of her sons (this she did between the feasts of Easter and Ascension) to be a servant to him, as the aforesaid Poitou asserted; the son was about 15 years of age; and afterwards she never saw him again.

"Theophania, the wife of Eonette le Charpentier, butcher, of the parish of St. Clement near Nantes, complained that Peter the son of Eonet le Dagaye, the grandchild of the complainant, ten years old or thereabouts, was lost two years ago, and from that time nothing was heard of him until the aforesaid Perrina Martin, *alias* la Peliszonne, nicknamed *la Meffraye*, confessed, as is said, that she had given him to the followers of M. de Rays.

"The wife of Peter Coupperie likewise complained that she had lost her two sons, one eight and the other nine years old.

"Johannes Magnet complained that he had lost a son. Wherefore the said complainants said that they suspected that the aforesaid M. de Rays and his accomplices were culpable and conscious of the loss and death of the aforesaid children."

The judges and those present and in authority were much moved by these scenes, and they declared that such crimes should not go unpunished, however high the rank of the accused, and they directed the bailiff to notify Gilles to appear before their tribunal the 8th of October to respond in their presence to the accusations against him. On that day more witnesses were introduced, but their depositions were not written out, or at least are not in the record.

The court was opened in the great audience chamber in due form and solemnity, at about nine o'clock in the morning. The audience was public, and the hall was crowded. Gilles was brought to the bar as a criminal, and required to plead. He carried a high head, looking around him disdainfully, as in the days of his power and strength. The bailiff recited that in accordance with the orders given to him, he had the possession of the body of Gilles de Retz, which he now presented before the court. Immediately the prosecutor arose, and proceeded verbally with the arraignment of the prisoner. It is to be remembered that the methods of procedure in the courts of that country are now, and were then, quite different from that of the common law courts.

After the oral statement of the crimes of which he was accused, the prosecutor called upon Gilles to plead, to which Gilles (also orally) declared his refusal, and demanded an appeal from the Bishop of Nantes and the Vice-Inquisitor,—supposed to be an appeal to the Archbishop at Tours or to the Pope himself. His appeal was refused immediately, and his plea demanded. Michelet (*Histoire de France*, vol. v., p. 210) justifies Gilles in his refusal to plead and his demand for an appeal. "For," he says, "one cannot deny that the judges before whom Gilles was to be tried were his enemies." Gilles seems, in making these demands, to have intended to use the law's delay more than to have had any special hope of being sustained by the higher courts.

It is remarkable, though, to consider the value attached by the court to Gilles's plea. It was evident that when he did plead, it would be a plea of "not guilty"; but this seemed to have had no effect upon the judges or upon their course of procedure. They appeared quite willing to permit the plea of "not guilty," but were determined to have a plea of some kind entered. It would be curious to trace the causes of this solicitude on the part of the judges. The filing of the plea may have been required for some purpose deeper than the appearance would indicate; possibly it stood in the stead of the present rule of law that requires the criminal to be arrested and brought before the court in order to give it jurisdiction. True, the party can, in France, be tried in his absence and convicted *in contumacion*; but this can only be done after the party shall have been arrested and filed his plea. In murder trials, no conviction can be had in the court of any civilised country until the proof shall be made of the *corpus delicti*. It would appear as though the importance of this plea was that it should be an evidence of the presence of the prisoner before the court. It may have been, in the eye of the law, a synecdoche, wherein a part stood for the whole,—a plea standing for the evidence of arrest and presence of the prisoner before the court,—which was necessary to give it jurisdiction over the case. However this may have been, the court manifested great determination to obtain the plea from Gilles. They gave him some days to consider the matter, but he replied at once that

> "none of the articles which you have presented against me are true except two things therein charged; the baptism that I have received, and the renunciation which I have sworn against the demon, his pomp and his works. I am now, and always have been, a true Christian."

Upon the receipt of this answer and defiance, the prosecutor became indignant. He offered his oath to support each and every one of the articles he had presented. Turning to Gilles, he demanded that he make the same oath, and in the same manner, that is, between the hands of the Bishop and the Vice-Inquisitor (*"entre les mains de l'évêque et du Vice-inquisiteur"*). This was demanded of him four different times—he was begged, pleaded with, implored, threatened, menaced with excommunication, but he remained strong in his refusal. What a strange thing is human nature! This man had committed the most fearful, inhuman, and base crimes,—crimes against the innocent and defenceless,—and yet, when brought to the bar of trial, he insisted he was a true Christian, and whatever else he might do or have done, he stood firm in his resolve not to take a false oath. He could commit murder times without number, and he seemed to consider the punishment for this relating only to the body. A false oath taken before God seemed to him to carry its punishment into the next world and to imperil his soul through eternity. He was willing to commit murder, but he was afraid to commit perjury.

The hearing was postponed until the 11th of October, to give the prosecutor time to prepare the information which should serve as an indictment and which had not yet been formally presented nor made a matter of record.

In the meantime, public attention must have been greatly attracted to the proceedings as they were progressing, and invitations went out to all persons who had lost children by abduction within the specified time and who had reason to suppose that the crime could be laid to Gilles, or his accomplices, to present themselves before the court and make their complaints.

Lemire relates (p. 39) this incident:

> "On the 10th of October, a herald-at-arms of the Duke of Brittany, bearing his livery, sounded the trumpet three times before the château and then, in a loud voice, demanded that any person having knowledge of the affair of Gilles de Retz was summoned to appear before the court and tell what he knew under pain of fine and imprisonment. No person responded to this appeal."

So great was the number appearing the next day in response to this notification that the court was unable to proceed with the trial, and consumed the 11th and 12th in its inquest, hearing and recording complaints of the many witnesses. As we have seen, these witnesses were presented before the judges, interrogated, and their statements taken down in the form of depositions, to the end that they might be included in the information against the prisoner. On October 13th, having finished this work, the court had the prisoner brought before it. The session of the court was held in public; the bench appears to have been filled with ecclesiastical dignitaries, many of them bishops from the neighbouring dioceses, with judges and lawyers; while below, an immense pressing, pushing, exasperated crowd of bereaved parents and friends, filled with emotion, added much to the excitement by their declarations of the losses they had sustained by the abduction of their dear children, and who filled the room with their cries against the perpetrator of the crimes by which they had been robbed of their loved ones.

The hour for opening was, as usual, nine o'clock. The first business was a return to the question of the plea to be filed by the accused. Gilles refused with greater hauteur than before, and pushed his refusal disdainfully, ending by becoming abusive of the judges and officers of the court, and conducting himself in a highly improper and insulting manner. The following extracts are from *Procès-verbal* of the audience (translated):

"Thursday, October 13, 1440.

"On the above-mentioned Thursday, the 13th day of October, there appeared in the court before the Lord Bishop of Nantes, etc., etc . . .

"Then the same Lord Bishop and the Vice-inquisitor and the aforesaid promoter, asked the aforesaid Egidius [Gilles], the accused, whether he wished to reply to the positions and articles against him, or whether he wished to say anything against them or to take any exception to them. He answered with pride and haughtiness that he wished to give no answer to the positions and articles, asserting that the aforesaid lords, the Bishop and Vice-inquisitor, were not his judges, and that he appealed from them, speaking irreverently and improperly.

"Moreover, the aforesaid Egidius, accused, then said that the aforesaid lords, the Bishop of Nantes and brother Jean Blouyn the vicar of the aforesaid Inquisitor, and all other ecclesiastical men were guilty of simony and were ribalds, and that he would rather be hanged by the neck than to answer before such ecclesiastics and judges, feeling it a grievance to have to appear before them, . . . and finally addressing the lord Bishop, he said in the vernacular, '*Je ne feroye rien pour vous comme évesque de Nantes.*' . . . Then under pain of excommunication he was asked to reply to the charges made against him, but he refused, saying that he wondered how it was that Petrus de l'Hospital, the President of Brittany, could have permitted that the ecclesiastics should be present at the accusation of such crimes against him, stating that he was a Christian and a Catholic, and that he was aware that such crimes would have been against faith.

"Then he was formally excommunicated, and it was decided to proceed with the trial, paying no attention to his declaration that he had appealed, since such appellation was merely in verbal declaration and not in writing, and since the enormity of the crimes of which he was accused demanded immediate attention."

No progress was made during the day, and the court was adjourned until the morrow, when the information would be completed and formally lodged against the accused.

The criminal proceedings in France, while different from those under the common law, yet still have some analogy therewith. There is no grand jury, but in its stead is an officer now called *juge d'instruction*. In this court no such special officer seems to have existed, but the duty of examining the witnesses, as done by the grand jury in the United States, was performed by the court itself, aided by the prosecutor. Instead of an indictment charging the crime as under the common law, an information is filed. The information is signed and presented in court by the prosecutor, and while being prepared is entirely within his control. He has, under the law, the power of our grand jury of charging, or refusing to charge, crimes; therefore the indictment is his. This information, instead of simply charging the crime directly, and in legal language, sets forth the history of the case, the jurisdiction of the court, the attending circumstances of the crime charged, and ends with the usual prayers for conviction and punishment.

The information against Gilles de Retz contained forty-nine articles, and charged him with three distinct crimes: (1) the crimes of abduction, violation, and murder of the infants named; (2) the crimes of magic and sorcery; (3) sacrilege in having violated the ecclesiastic immunity of the chapel of Saint Étienne-de-Mer-Morte. The information was divided into three parts. The first fourteen of the forty-nine articles were occupied with stating the jurisdiction of the court, that is to say, that Jean de Malestroit was the Bishop of Nantes, that he was properly and legally appointed as such, that he was under his superior, the archbishop, whose ecclesiastical province or cathedral was located at Tours; then followed the power, authority, and right to sit, of Jean Blouyn, the Vice-Inquisitor; then the declaration of the nativity of Gilles de Retz, his residence in the diocese of, and duty owed to, the Bishop of Nantes; a declaration of the ecclesiastical authority of the Bishop within his diocese over the château of Machecoul and the chapel of Saint Étienne-de-Mer-Morte and, in fine, a complete statement of all necessary authority over the accused, and this part finished with the declaration that all things herein set forth were true, notorious, manifest, and within the knowledge of all and every person.

The second part of the information comprised articles fifteen to forty-one. Article fifteen was a general statement of all the crimes charged against Gilles and his accomplices. The names of the accused were first stated: Gilles de Retz, Gilles de Sillé, Roger de Briqueville, Henriet Griart, Étienne Corrillaud, *alias* Poitou, Andrea Bouchet, Jean Rossignol, Robin Romulart, called Spadin, Huguet de Bremont, and the crimes charged were the murder of infants, killed, dismembered, burned, treated in an inhuman manner. Then there were the immolation damnable of the bodies of these infants offered to the demon as a sacrifice; consultation with the demon, odious conduct, frightful abomination, brutal debauches, and, taken together, a catalogue of crimes, a luxury of offences that exhausted the prosecutor to qualify in proper terms, and which, before a mixed assembly, could only be pronounced decently in Latin and not in vulgar language.

He told of the excitement, dread, fear, of the people; the public clamour that had sprung up from one end of the country to the other; how it at last settled around the château of Machecoul, and that every time an abduction took place some one of the accomplices of Gilles had been discovered in the neighbourhood. In making this part of his accusation, the prosecutor became filled with emotion, excited in his address, and eloquent in his words. He described the conduct and feelings of the people, and especially of the stricken parents, of their cries (*clamosa*, for his first presentation and reading of the information was in Latin), the loud lamentations (*lamentabile*), the immense sorrow (*plurimum dolorosa*), the accusing insinuations of the people; he showed the innumerable persons of both sexes and all conditions, both in the cities and in the diocese of Nantes, (*præcedentibus vocibus quam plurimarum personarum utriusque sexus*), who, bowed down by the weight of their grief and fright, had appealed to justice and to heaven with howls and cries (*ululantium*), and had presented their complaints together before the seat of justice, their visages bathed in tears (*conquerentium et plangentium*), for the loss of their sons and daughters, bringing to the Bishop, the commissioners, and the prosecutors the authority of their tears and their griefs in support of this accusation.

Article sixteen commenced with the charge of the crime of conjuration and invocation of demons. Over this the prosecutor also became eloquent. His accusation was of an infraction of ecclesiastical law, and he dealt largely with the law of the Church; his charges abounded in quotations from the Bible (Fourth and Thirty-ninth Psalms), adjurations from holy men, and was filled with many brave and eloquent words in description and denunciation of the abominable crime of black magic, conjuration, and sorcery. He takes up the Italian priests from their respective places in their native country, and brings them along until they are joined to Gilles in Brittany. In the articles alleging crimes against infants, in article twenty-seven, the accusation says, "and the number of victims is upward of one hundred and forty, and possibly more. The articles of the accusation following set forth the details of all these horrors; the action, conduct, and aid of the familiars of Gilles and his accomplices; when, where, for whom, and by whom the infants were taken, and their respective fates. These were all set forth in great detail and with great particularity, and article forty-one closes with the words: "These are the crimes which make Gilles de Retz infamous, a heretic, an apostate, an idolate, and a *relaps.*"

Articles forty-two to forty-seven were occupied with a recapitulation of the crimes committed by Gilles and his accomplices, and in article forty-nine he concludes with the assurance that by such crimes and by such offences the accused had incurred the sentence of excommunication and all other pains which follow the punishment to be assessed against such culpable of being *auruspex et ariolus*, the doers of evil deeds, the conjurors of evil spirits, their aiders and abettors, their friends, their dependants, and, finally, all those who have delivered themselves over to magic and the prohibited art. That the accused had fallen into heresy, that they were guilty of *relaps*, that they had offended the majesty of God, which was infinitely worse than the offence against the priests; they had incurred, consequently, the penalties for crimes against His Majesty Divine; they had broken the commands of the Decalogue, the laws of the Church; they had sown among the faithful Christians the most dangerous errors; finally, that they were rendered culpable of crimes as enormous as they were hideous, all of which were in the jurisdiction of the Bishop of Nantes. And in the closing sentences the prosecutor demands that he shall be admitted now to make proof of what he has advanced, and this he will do, so he promises, without further superfluity, reserving only the right to add, to correct, to change, to diminish, to interpret, and to put in order and produce any new matters if they shall be necessary at the time and place convenient; and he demands the application of the punishment due for this crime. The prosecutor admitted that certain of the crimes set forth in the information were not within the jurisdiction of the ecclesiastical court, and that they would have to be remitted to the secular court if punishment was expected.

Gilles de Retz interrupted the reading of the information many times, making denials in favour of himself, blaming his judges, and denouncing the prosecutors. Everybody seems to have preserved his temper except Gilles, and at the close of the reading of the information, the judges turned to him and demanded his formal plea to the various accusations against him. Gilles remained obstinate and refused to plead, and demanded an appeal to the higher court. His conduct during the reading was such as to destroy any sympathy the judges may have had. Bishops and judges are but men, and it was too much to expect that the human side of the court would hear, unmoved, this abuse and contumely heaped upon it.

Gilles's continued refusal to plead gave the prosecutor and court an opportunity to exercise their legal power, and the prosecutor demanded a decree of excommunication against Gilles for his contempt in this behalf committed. This was an interlocutory order, intended to correct the faults of Gilles during the trial. It was useless to imprison him, for he was already a prisoner; it was useless to threaten him with any other pains or penalties applied to his physical body; therefore, the court, using the only other power it had as an ecclesiastical body, issued its decree of excommunication, the only thunder it could fulminate against him.

It is a curious commentary upon human nature, and throws a side light, not simply upon the ecclesiastical courts, but also upon the human nature of that day, that Gilles, who had committed all the crimes in the calendar, and deserved death a thousand times if he had had that many lives; who seemed to have no fear of any punishment inflicting physical pain or discomfort in this world, yet was so filled with dread of punishment in the next world, arising from the decree of excommunication which he believed and feared would deprive him of the solace of his religion and the benefit of the vicarious intercession of his holy Mother Church that, as we shall see, it produced the greatest effect upon him and was of the greatest efficacy in changing his course.

The decree of excommunication having been passed upon Gilles de Retz, a postponement was ordered until the Saturday following, October 15th.

At the next sitting Gilles had had two or three days in which to think over his condition. Brought to the bar, the Court put to him the original question, "Do you recognise us as your legitimate judges?" To which question, to the suprise of everyone who heard him, Gilles, who had heretofore been so proud and disdainful in all his refusals to respond affirmatively to this question, spoke out, "Yes; I recognise the Court as at present constituted. I have committed crimes, and they have been within the limits of this diocese." With words of humility and regret, his voice broken with emotion, with tears in his eyes, he demanded pardon of the Bishop and Vice-Inquisitor for the words he had spoken so harshly against them.

The Bishop, who had heretofore been dignified, reserved, severe, as became a judge in the trial of a case, on hearing these words of submission and request for pardon, turned the other side of his character towards the repentant. He then became the priest whose duty was to pardon, comfort, and console erring and sinful men; and when Gilles prayed that his decree of excommunication be revoked, that he should be re-admitted to the fold of the Church and again be given the comforts of his religion, the Bishop granted the prayers, and received him again into the Church, giving him words of comfort and good cheer.

When this scene was finished, the prosecutor asked for the progress of the trial in the usual way. Gilles raised no objection, and expressed his willingness to enter his plea and take oath to speak the truth in all things whereof he was accused. The information was read to him at length in the Latin language, and explained, section by section, in the common French. Gilles responded to the first fourteen articles, admitting in succession the powers of the Bishop and of the Vice-Inquisitor, the lawful constitution of the court, and that he was a member of the Church, and that the *venue*, as laid, was within the jurisdiction. Being further interrogated, he, however, denied all dealings with the Evil One, all performances of magic, all attempts at sorcery, or that he had ever, either by himself or by another, sought to have communication with the Evil One, or to invoke his power in any way in order to obtain riches, power, or long life. He admitted that he had once possessed a book that treated of alchemy and of the invocation of demons; that he had obtained it from a soldier who had been thrown in prison at Angers; that he had talked with the soldier upon that subject, but had done nothing more—he had returned the book.

The record recounts how, at this period in the trial, the prosecutor demanded of Gilles that they two, in order to be on equal terms, should take the oath to speak the truth. They advanced together, the prosecutor and the defendant, and putting their left hands between the hands of the Bishop and of the Vice-Inquisitor, their right hands bearing upon the Holy Evangel, they took together the oath "To speak the truth and nothing but the truth," as to the matter before the court.

This ceremony over, the formal plea of "not guilty" was entered by Gilles. Then came the introduction of witnesses, who were, Henri Griard, Étienne Corrillaud, *alias* Poitou, François Prelati, Demontie Cativo, Eustache Blanchet, Étienne of St. Malo, Steophanie Etiennette, widow of Robert Branchee, and Perrina Martin, surnamed *la Meffraye.* They were all brought to the bar by Robert Guillaumet, the bailiff, and appeared on the side of the prosecutor and against the defendant. The oath which the witnesses took is given in substance in the record. They were sworn between the hands of the Bishop and the Vice-Inquisitor, as Gilles and the prosecutor had been, and their oath was that neither favour, nor resentment, nor fear, nor hate, nor friendship, nor relationship, should have any part in their words; and they put aside every spirit of party and all personal affection, having regard only for truth and justice.

The judges announced to Gilles the privileges of cross-examination, putting the questions himself if he desired to do so, for, be it understood, usually in criminal trials under the civil law, especially in France, the questions, whether they be by the prosecutor or by the accused, have to be handed up, and are put by the presiding justice. But as it is usual for the witnesses to proceed and tell their story without interrogation, Gilles declared his willingness to have the regular course pursued, and that he would leave the matter to the conscience of the Court. This being done, the witnesses were removed; for, be it understood, by no court practice in France are the witnesses who have not testified permitted to remain while others are giving testimony. The presence of Gilles's accomplices as witnesses against him must have given him an awful shock. As soon as the witnesses had left the court-room, it seems that the condition of affairs presented themselves to Gilles in their true light, and showed him his serious and compromising situation. He was moved to great emotion, whether of remorse or fear cannot now be said. He demanded, in supplicating tones, that the revocation of the decree of excommunication should be in writing, not simply by oral decree.

It would appear from such of the history of this great criminal as we have, that the only thing which produced any emotion in him and caused him to exhibit fear or dread of his position was this decree of excommunication. The Bishop was in his forgiving mood, he had resumed his *rôle* of priest, and, very properly, he consented to do in writing what he had already done verbally, and the decree of excommunication was revoked.

The court adjourned until the Monday thereafter, the 17th of October, when it was expected that the introduction of evidence would begin. The examination was taken either orally (*viva voce*), before the court, or by the clerks, or *greffiers*, who acted as examiners, or notaries, and reduced the testimony to writing, reporting it or its substance to the court. De Alneto, Jo. Parvi, and G. Lesne were *greffiers*, and took most of the testimony for the ecclesiastical court; while de Touscheronde did the same for the civil court, and it was reported under their respective certificates.

October 17th was occupied with witnesses proving the crime of sacrilege committed on the chapel of Saint Étienne-de-Mer-Morte. On the 19th the witnesses were examined touching the crime of abduction of infants. This interests us more than the other, and therefore we follow it with the names of the witnesses: Professor Jean de Pencortic, Jean Andilanrech, André Seguin, Pierre Vimain, Jean Orienst, Jean Brient, Jean Le Veill, Jean Picard, Guillaume Michel, Pierre Drouet, Eutrope Chardavoine, Robert Guillaumet (Doctor), Robin Riou, Jacques Tennecy, and Jean Letournours. All of these were sworn, as before, to tell the truth without consideration of prayers, or recompense, or fear, or favour, or hate, or resentment, or friendship, or acquaintance's sake. Gilles again declined to cross-examine the witnesses; he declared his willingness to abide by their conscientious declarations.

On the 20th of October the court was convened for the purpose of hearing the depositions, and Gilles was asked, with many questions, what response he had to make. He continually said he had none: nothing to say, nothing to ask of the witnesses, and no witnesses of his own to introduce. Practically, he made no controversy over the testimony against him.

The ecclesiastical court was equal to a court of the Inquisition. Two hundred or more years of practice by the Inquisition in prosecution of heresy had served to formulate rules of practice. And here is introduced one of the curiosities of human nature manifested in trials of justice when they are started in a given direction. Recurring to remarks concerning the legal necessity of obtaining a plea to the indictment or information, in order, possibly, to show the presence of the accused, and speculating upon that as the origin of the theory of the common law requiring the personal presence of the accused in order to give the court jurisdiction to try the case, and the proof of the *corpus delicti* in order to convict, it seems proper that a similar course of procedure and reasoning should prevail in cases of heresy, an offence which dealt so largely with matters of belief; therefore, the ecclesiastical court, or the Inquisitor, whether established as a court or not, deemed it necessary to appeal to the inner consciousness and the private knowledge of the accused in regard to his belief, and to that end put questions that demanded an answer.

As a matter of course, the prisoner, if a heretic, would refuse to answer because he would not convict himself, and hence grew up (this is only a suggestion of the author) a system which seems horrible and revolting to all lawyers; that is, the application of torture to compel the prisoner to make the necessary answer. No other punishment could be provided, for the accused was already a prisoner, and being punished as such. As nothing in the way of legal punishment further than imprisonment would be visited upon him, the Inquisition fell upon torture as a means of extorting a confession, and thus it forced from the unwilling lips of the accused a declaration of his belief. This would soon extend to include all his knowledge concerning matters at issue; and when he should declare himself innocent, however true it might be, the torture could be applied again and again, harder and greater, until the power of resistance on the part of the accused was overcome, and he would give up because of his inability to resist further.

So it appeared in the case of Gilles. The witnesses had testified to everything necessary to be proved; Gilles had admitted the jurisdiction and the *corpus delicti*, had practically admitted his immediate and direct connivance and assistance in the various abductions, as well as the sacrilege; still, on his refusal to proceed further, the prosecutor demanded the application of torture.

It was, according to our ideas, a lamentable condition of the course of justice when the application of the torture should have been so common a proceeding that, on demand of the prosecutor, it would be allowed by the court, even when the guilt of the prisoner was beyond dispute. This seems to have been the course of the court in the case of Gilles, and the petition for torture, as made by the prosecutor, was allowed by the court, and the next day set for its application.

"Et tunc idem promotor dixit quod, attenta confessione dicti Egidii, rei, productionibus testium et eorum dictis depositionibus satis constabat de intencione sua in causa et hujusmodi, sed nichilominus, ad veritatem lacius elucidandam et perscrutandam, torturam seu questionem dicto Egidio, reo, per eosdem dominos episcopum Nannetensem et Fratrem Johannem Blouyn, judices, et ipsum questionari debere, instanter postulavit.

"Qui quidem domini episcopus et vicarius dicti inquisitoris, prius habito per eos super his omnibus consilio cum peritis, premissis consideratis, decreverunt questionem sive torturam dicto Egidio *de Rays*, et eum torturam pati, ipsumque Egidium, reum, torturis sive questionibus subici debere."

It was said that the instrument of torture had already been put in place, and for the convenience of all parties the prosecutor had chosen the hall adjoining that occupied by Gilles, to the end that the torture could be applied with as little trouble as possible, and whatever might be the result of it that Gilles could be properly attended to in case of need. On this demand of the prosecutor for torture, and its allowance by the judges, Gilles's courage left him; he became frightened, turned pale and trembled. So full of fear and terror was he, as scarcely to be able to speak intelligently. He threw himself at the feet of his judges and, in broken accents, with cries and sobs, besought and supplicated them not to put him to this test, making all kinds of promises as to what he would do in order to escape torture.

He prayed for leave to make confession of his crimes, and to have the Bishop of Saint-Brieuc assigned for that purpose.

It was agreed that the judge, Pierre l'Hospital, the President of Brittany, should sit with the Bishop to hear the proposed confession, and that the session should be held at two o'clock that afternoon. Gilles agreed to this, as he would have agreed to anything else, and he promised to make a clean breast of the whole affair. But as an evidence of the terror with which he contemplated the torture, he demanded (this seems to have been his only condition) that his examination and confession should be taken in a hall as distant as possible from that of the torture. The court agreed to this proposition at once, and the two officials named were assigned the duty. The secretaries, or clerks of the court, acting respectively for these high functionaries, were Jean Parvi for the ecclesiastical court, and Jean de Touscheronde for the civil court.

It is said that Gilles's confession before these two representatives of the ecclesiastical and civil powers was made in public, where everybody who desired could enter and hear. This confession of the same day is headed, in the records (archives), *extra-judiciare*, for what reason is unknown; but, as there was a fuller, and apparently a judicial, confession made by him the next day, which will be given at length, the confession *extra-judiciare* is omitted, the incident only being mentioned.

The President of Brittany, Pierre l'Hospital, undertook the interrogation of Gilles. He took up first the crimes against the infants, their abduction and murder, and went through that with great minutiæ, pushing it to all details; then the same with regard to sorcery and the invocation of demons; the bloody sacrifices that had been offered to the Evil One, as had been in evidence so many days. Pressed to tell where this commenced, Gilles said it was at the château of Champtocé, that the time was so long ago that he had forgotten and was unable to identify it, except that it was in the year in which his grandfather, Jean de Craon, had died. "Who gave to you, and how did you get, the idea of committing these crimes?" "No one; my own imagination drove me to do so. The thought was my own, and

I have nothing to which to attribute it except my own desire for knowledge of evil."

It appears, from the report of the case, that the President of Brittany did not believe these statements of Gilles's to be possible. He was so much astonished to hear this declaration that he pushed the examination with great detail, and insisted upon fuller and more specific answers. He approached Gilles sometimes from the legal side, sometimes from the ecclesiastical; sometimes he threatened him with the punishment of the secular arm, at other times he pleaded with him and held out the offers of pardon from the Lord Jesus Christ; and by virtue of all these, he besought Gilles to go back over the words which he had spoken, to make a truthful and honest avowal of the causes which had led him to the commission of these frightful crimes.

There were three languages employed in these proceedings; probably all three were spoken by the higher orders: the Latin by the ecclesiastical authorities, and that language was employed by the ecclesiastical court; then the French language, which was foreign to Brittany, but which probably Gilles and all those concerned in the trial understood; while as for the common people, doubtless their knowledge was confined to the Breton language. The confession of Gilles, reduced to writing by the clerk's secretary, not verbatim, nor pretending to be so, but to have been written out only in substance, as is done in the case of testimony before an examiner or notary who employs longhand.

While the President was pushing this investigation and cross-examination so far, to the visible annoyance and great trouble of Gilles, he cried out in French: "Alas, Monseigneur, you torment yourself and me also, both of us, unnecessarily!" "No," replied the President of Brittany, "I do not torment myself; but I am astonished at what you have said, and I am scarcely content with it. My only desire is to have you tell the truth concerning the causes which I have so oftentimes asked you." Responded Gilles: "There is no other cause; I have told you the truth and everything as it happened; *Je vous ay dit de plus grans choses que n'est cest cy, et assez pour faire mourir dix milles hommes* (I have said to you all things as they are, and enough to kill ten thousand men)." Then the President gave over interrogating him, and accepted his declaration as true. He was sent back to his chamber, and his accomplice, François Prelati, the Italian priest, chemist, and alchemist, was brought out.

Transcription of the next page, being sample (photograph by the author) of a Latin manuscript of the Record in the process against Gilles de Retz, from the Archives of Loire-Inférieure, Nantes, a page of his (extra-judicial) confession.

"hoc facere illo anno quo defunctus avunculus suus dominus *de la Suze* decessit.

"Item, interrogatus per ipsum dominum presidentem quis eundem reum advisavit, consuluit vel instruxit ad predicta facinora facienda, respondit quod hec de se ipso imaginatus fuit, cogitavit, fecit, et perpetravit, nemine consulente seu advertente aut ipsum ad hoc introducente, sed ex proprio suo sensu et capite ac pro complicencia et delectacione suis libidinosis explendis, et non pro quacumque alia intencione seu fine, predicta peccata, scelera et delicta fecerat et commiserat. Et, cum dictus dominus presidens, admirans, ut dicebat, qualiter ipse reus hec premissa scelera et delicta de se ipso et nemine instigante fecisset, ipsum reum iterum summasset ut ex quo motivo seu intencione et ad quem finem dictorum puerorum occisionem, cum eis commixtionem seu pollucionem, et ipsorum cadaverum combustionem, et reliqua scelera et peccata predicta fecisset, vellet ipse reus, ad sue consciencie, ipsum verissimiliter accusantis, exonerationem, et pro venia clementissimi Redemptoris inde super commissis facilius obtinenda, plenius declarare: tune idem reus, quasi quodammodo indignatus super tam sollicita et exacta inquiscione dicti domini presidentis, dixit eidem verba que secuntur gallice: '*Helas, Monseigneur, vous vous tourmentez et moy avecques*': cui reo dicenti dominus presidens ita dixit gallice: '*Je ne me tourmente point, mais je suis moult esmerveillé de ce que vous me dites et ne m'en puis bonnement contenter. Ainczois, je desire et vouldroye par vous en savoir la pure verité pour les causes que je vous ay ja souventes foiz dictes.*' Cui domino presidenti ipse reus tunc respondit, hec dicens gallice: '*Vrayement, il n'y avoit autre cause, fin, ne intencion que ce que je vous ay dit: je vous ay dit de plus grans choses que n'est cest cy, et assez pour faire mourir dix mille hommes.*' Qui quidem dominis presidens tunc omisit ipsum reum."

Facsimile of folio page from archives of trial at Nantes. Confession of Gilles de Retz.

Prelati had already confessed to the invocation of evil spirits, and that he had made offerings of the blood and of the members of an infant. Being interrogated, he made his formal confession, also reduced to writing, but it turned out that this was only a repetition of an informal confession, so excited no great surprise. The interrogators seemed more interested in the invocation of demons than in the abduction and murder of the infants. Gilles and François were brought together before the judges and the Bishop, and upon the conclusion of the séance they were sent back to their respective prisons. On parting, Gilles turned towards François, and sobbing, embraced him with sorrow, and addressed to him his last words: "Adieu, François, my friend. Never again will we see each other in this world. I pray that you may have good patience and hope in God, and that we will see each other in the great joy of Paradise. Pray to God for me and I will pray for you."

They tenderly embraced each other and then separated, never to see each other again. This scene happened, and these two confessions were made, before the two officers in private audience, in chambers, as it were.

On the next day, Saturday, October 22d, the *judicial* confession of Gilles was made, and presented before the court. It is herewith given in the *procès-verbal* of the session:

Translation of the Confession of Gilles de Retz.

"On Saturday, the 22d of the aforesaid month of October, the aforesaid master Guillermus Champeillon, promoter, prosecutor, on the one hand, and the aforesaid Gilles de Retz, defendant, on the other, personally repaired to the trial before the before-mentioned lords, the reverend Father, the Lord Bishop of Nantes, and Brother John Blouyn, vicar of the said Inquisitor, who had taken their seats in the tribunal there in the aforesaid place at the vesper hour for the rendition of justice. And acting in accordance with the assignment of the day of trial on the motion of the said prosecutor, the afore-mentioned lords, the Bishop of

Nantes and Brother John Blouyn, vicar of the aforesaid Inquisitor, asked the aforesaid Gilles, defendant, whether he wished to say anything or make any opposition or objection to (the evidence or charges) produced or maintained in this case and similar cases. The defendant, indeed, said and replied that he did not wish to say anything, and fully and of his own accord, and with great compunction and bitterness of heart, as was evident at first sight, and with copious shedding of tears, confessed that the already recorded [charges], elsewhere, as [mentioned] above, extra-judicially confessed to, [namely] in his room in presence of the aforesaid reverend Father, the Lord Bishop of Saint-Brieuc, of master Pierre de l'Hospital, the President, of John de Touscheronde and of John Parvi, as well as all and everything contained and described in the articles inserted above, will be and are true. And adding to his extra-judicial confession already inserted and not receding from it, which the same accused wished right here [to be considered] as repeated and declared, and as he stated, rectifying the defects if perchance he had omitted anything in it, and moreover more fully declaring and enlarging, he freely confessed some things contained in a summary form in certain of the afore-mentioned articles, and said, to wit, that he had committed and perpetrated very many other greater and more enormous crimes and sins against God and His commandments than are contained in the articles already inserted, from the beginning of his iniquitous youth against God and His writings, and that he had offended our Saviour Himself by the evil training he had had in his boyhood in which he had endeavoured to perform whatever pleased him with unbridled rein and had given himself to everything illicit; and imploring those present who had children, that they have their sons brought up and trained in their youth and boyhood in religious instruction and virtue.

"After this confession, as it is already stated, judicially given and made by the aforesaid Gilles de Retz, the accused, of the contents in the aforesaid articles, and, [after] that extra-judicial

[confession] repeated and declared, the same accused moreover
made another confession of the following tenor, separate and
apart, in the presence of the reverend Father in Christ, Lord
John Prigencii, Bishop of Saint-Brieuc and the nobleman Pierre
de l'Hospital, the above-mentioned President of Brittany, and of
John Abbatis, the shield-bearer, and of me, John Parvi, notary
public and general examiner of the ecclesiastical court of Nantes,
a second of the secretaries of [this] cause and of similar causes,
and of John de Touscheronde, also secretary of the civil court of
the same place, concerning the afore-mentioned perpetrations,
crimes, and sins, embracing the vices and sins mentioned . . . [all]
iniquitously committed by him: not only as much as is perhaps
contained in the aforewritten articles already freely confessed
to, by Gilles himself, the accused, and in order that said secret
confession be more widely published, the same Gilles, defendant,
thought it proper that, without departing from the said extra-
judicial confession made by him concerning the said charges, but
rather to strengthen and corroborate it, the confession itself be
published in the vernacular for the benefit of the people and all
then and there assisting, of whom the greater part knew no Latin;
that, however, an introductory remark be added informing those
present that the culprit submitted to this general revelation of
his guilt in order by the shame this publication and confession of
such crimes committed by him would cause him, the more easily
to obtain from God pardon and remission for his sins and to have
wiped away the transgression committed by him. [He wished
the public to know] that during his youth he had always been
tenderly reared, had committed as much as in him lay and with
nothing to check his inclination, all the evil deeds he could, had
centred all his hope, intention, and work upon the commission of
illicit and shameful deeds and had employed [his hope, intention,
and work] in unlawful acts by perpetrating said crimes—most
earnestly beseeching and exhorting the fathers, mothers, friends,
and relatives of all youths to guide their charges along the paths
of honesty by setting them a good example and instilling into

107

them sound doctrine, and to chastise every fault against good morals to save them from the snares into which he himself had fallen. By this secret confession which was examined and publicly read in court in the presence of the said Gilles, defendant, and approved by Gilles himself, the defendant, the said Gilles de Retz, the defendant, manifested of his own accord before all present and confessed that he, led by passion and the delight he took in satisfying his carnal appetite—of which mention will be made later on—had stolen or caused to be stolen very many boys—the number he could not remember; that he had put these boys to death and caused them to be killed and that with them he had committed crimes and sins . . . [that he had killed] these boys, sometimes himself with his own hand, and sometimes through the agency of others and especially the above-mentioned Gilles de Sillé, the Lord Roger Briqueville, soldier, Henriet et Poitou, Rossignol and Little Robin, by various kinds and modes of torture, some by the amputation and separation of their heads from their bodies using daggers or poniards and knives; others, however, with sticks or other implements for striking by beating them on the head with violent blows; others again by tying them with cords and fastening them to some door or iron hook . . . in his own room that they might be strangled and languish. [He continued] that with these boys even whilst languishing . . . and after their death he took delight in kissing, in gazing intently at those who had the more beautifully formed heads and in cruelly opening or causing to be opened their bodies that he might see their interior, and that frequently, whilst these boys were dying, he would sit on their stomachs and take great pleasure in seeing them thus dying, and that he used to laugh heartily at the sight with the said Corrillaud and Henriet. The corpses he caused afterwards to be burned and reduced to ashes by the same Corrillaud and Henriet and others.

"Interrogated concerning the places where he had perpetrated the afore-mentioned crimes and at what time he had begun to do these things and concerning the number of those killed after this manner, he answered and said that [first he had done so] in the Château de Champtocé and from that year on in which lived the lord de la Suze, the maternal uncle of said defendant; that in this place he had killed and caused to be killed very many boys—the number he could not remember— . . . the aforesaid Gilles de la Sillé alone knowing of the matter at that time; but that afterwards the aforesaid Roger de Briqueville and then Henriet, Stephen Corrillaud (*alias* Poitou), Rossignol, and Robin became successively his accomplices and sharers in these crimes. And he said that the bones both of the heads and the bodies of the boys killed in the aforesaid Château de Champtocé, as has been stated, which had been thrown into the lower apartment of a certain tower of that castle, he himself, defendant, produced from that spot, placed in coffins or chests, and transported by water to the place and castle of Machecoul aforesaid, burned there and caused to be reduced to ashes; that also, in the same place of Machecoul, he himself, defendant, seized, killed, and caused to be stolen and killed many other boys in large numbers—how many he could not recollect; and that, again, in the manor called la Suze, of Nantes, which he, Gilles, defendant, then owned, he had similarly killed and caused to be killed, burned, and reduced to ashes many other boys of whom he could not remember the numbers . . . The same Gilles de Retz, defendant, narrated and confessed that all misdeeds, crimes, and transgressions above mentioned he committed and criminally perpetrated of his own free will and accord alone, for the purpose of satisfying his evil and iniquitous complacency and pleasure and not out of any other motive or intention, with no one to urge or advise him, defendant, or even to call to his attention such thoughts.

"Furthermore, he declared and confessed that, after the expiration of a year and a half, the Lord Eustace Blanchet aforesaid summoned the aforesaid François Prelati from the country of Florence in Lombardy and invited him to the same Gilles, defendant, for the purpose of invoking demons according to the intention of the defendant, and that François, summoned to the same defendant, informed him that he, François, had discovered in the country whence he had come means of conjuring up a certain spirit by the aid of incantations, which spirit had promised him, François, that he would cause a certain demon called *Barron* to come to him, François, as often as the same François might desire.

"Likewise, the same Gilles de Retz declared and confessed that the same François made several invocations of demons in compliance with a command of himself, defendant, both during his absence and sometimes when he was present, and that he himself, defendant, was in person present at three such invocations of François who made them: One in the Château Tiffauges, another in Bourgneuf de Retz, aforesaid, and that concerning the third aforesaid invocation he did not recall in which place it was made. And he added that the said Lord Eustace knew that the said François was making such invocations, but that the same Lord Eustace was not present at these invocations, since neither the defendant himself nor François would permit him to be present at the incantations, as the same Lord Eustace had an indirect, evil, and restless tongue.

"Besides, the selfsame defendant declared and confessed that during these invocations there were traced as characters on the ground figures of a circle and a cross, and that the same François possessed a book which he had carried about his person, as he used to say, which contained many names of demons and formulæ for the making of such conjurations and invocations of demons, which names and formulæ he, defendant, could not remember; that the said François held and read this book for about two hours during and for each invocation; but that at none of his own conjurations or invocations the defendant saw or noticed any devil, and that none spoke to him, at which he, defendant, was much displeased and vexed.

"Afterwards the same defendant declared and confessed that after a certain invocation made by the said François during the absence of the said defendant, the same François on his return

from that very invocation informed the said defendant that
he, François, had seen and addressed the said *Barron*, who had
told him, François, that he, *Barron*, did not appear to the said
defendant because the defendant had deceived *Barron* regarding
some promises read by the said defendant to the said *Barron*
and because he had not fulfilled his promise. Hearing this, the
said defendant bade François ask the same devil what he wished
to receive from the said defendant and that whatever the same
Barron might wish to receive and ask of the said defendant,
he, the defendant, would give him—except his soul and life
and provided the devil would give and grant him, defendant,
whatsoever he would ask. The defendant added then that it had
been and was his intention to ask and acquire from the same
devil knowledge, riches, and power, by the possession and aid of
which he, defendant, would be enabled to return to his former
state of dominion and power; and that, afterward, the same
François told the said defendant that he had conversed with the
devil and that the said devil, among other things, required and
wished that the defendant present to him, the devil, a limb or
limbs of some infant. That the defendant, later, delivered to the
said François the hand, heart, and eyes of an infant to be offered
and given to the same devil by the said François, on the part of
the said defendant.

"Again, the said Gilles de Retz, defendant, declared and
confessed that before he, defendant, took part in the second of
the three aforesaid invocations at which he assisted in person as is
stated above, he [defendant] wrote and signed with his own hand
a grant . . . to the bottom of which he appended his name in the
vernacular, videlicet 'Gilles,' the contents of which, however, he
does not remember; which grant he composed and signed with
the intention of handing it over to the devil if and while he came,
conjured or summoned by the said François, and this he did
acting upon the advice of the said François, who previously had
told the defendant that he, the defendant, must hand over that
grant to the devil as soon as the spirit should come or approach:

111

and that during this invocation the defendant continually held that grant in his hand waiting to hear the promise and agreement concerning which François and the devil should come to terms regarding the matters which the said defendant was to promise and to do for the devil, who did not appear or speak with them so that, accordingly, the defendant did not ever hand over the mentioned grant.

"Again, said defendant declared and confessed that he himself sent the aforesaid Stephen Corrillaud, *alias* Poitou, along with the said François, as François was one night going out to make one of the aforesaid invocations. These two on their return, drenched by a heavy rainstorm, stated to the said defendant that during the invocation nothing had come to them.

"Again, the said defendant declared and confessed that wishing to assist at a certain invocation which François proposed to make, the latter expressed his dissatisfaction that Gilles should then be present at the invocation. Returning from the invocation, he told the said defendant that, if he had been present at the invocation, he would have run great risk, for at that invocation there came and appeared a serpent to the same François which filled him with great fear: hearing this the said defendant after taking and causing to be carried near him a particle of the True Cross in his possession, expressed a longing to go to the spot of the said invocation where the said François claimed to have seen the reptile. This, however, he did not in deference to François's prohibition.

"Again, the same Gilles de Retz, defendant, declared and confessed that at one of the three aforesaid invocations at which he assisted, as is stated above, the said François informed him that he, François, had seen the said *Barron* who showed him a large quantity of gold and, among other things, an ingot of gold; but the said defendant said he had seen neither the devil nor the said ingot but only a sort of gold-leaf [*auripelli aurum-pellis* (?)] under the form of a leaf of gold which he, defendant, did not touch.

"Again, the said defendant declared and confessed subsequently that when he was recently at the court of the most illustrious Lord and Prince, the Lord of Brittany, in the Canton Jocelin, of the diocese of Maclovia he, defendant, caused to be killed several boys furnished him by the aforesaid Henriet, . . . in the above stated manner.

"Again, the same defendant declared and confessed that the said François, acting on the instigation and during the absence of the defendant, performed there, viz. at Jocelin, an invocation of the demons, at which he learned that nothing took place.

"Again, the said defendant, setting out from Bituris, dismissed the said François at the same Château de Tiffauges, asking him meanwhile and during the absence of the said defendant to attend and devote himself diligently to such incantations, and to repeat to the defendant whatsoever he would learn, do, and think in that regard; and that François wrote to him, the absent defendant, as has been stated, in cipher, called in French *par paroles couvertes*, that his transactions went on satisfactorily and that at this time the same François sent him, the defendant, a certain object after the manner of an ointment lodged in a silver capsule and purse (*bursa*) also made of silver, the said François writing at the same time to the aforesaid defendant that this was an entirely precious object and advising the said defendant furthermore in his letter to guard the object solicitously. The defendant, giving credence to this admonition of the said François, hung the object with the above-mentioned *bursa* about his neck and wore it for several days thus suspended; afterwards, however, the defendant removed the object from his neck and threw it away, as he discovered that it would not in the least benefit him.

"Again, the same defendant declared and confessed that the said François once told him that the aforesaid *Barron* bade the defendant feed, in the name of the said *Barron*, three poor men on three great feasts, which the defendant did on a certain All Saints' Day, and only once.

"Interrogated why he thus kept in his house and about his person the afore-mentioned François, he made answer that François was clever, valuable to him, and pleasant company because he spoke Latin beautifully and charmingly, and because, furthermore, he showed himself anxious concerning the proper administration of his affairs.

"Again, the said defendant declared and confessed that, after the last festival of St. John the Baptist, a certain handsome youth who stayed with a man named Rodigus dwelling in the aforesaid Place Bourgneuf de Retz, was one night brought to him, defendant, as he dwelt in the same place, by the said Henriet and Stephen Corrillaud, *alias* Poitou, and that during that night the defendant . . . caused him to be killed and to be burned near Machecoul.

"Again, the said defendant declared and confessed that, news having reached him that the soldiers of the municipal fortress of Paluau strove to put to death the captain of the fortress, St. Stephen de Mala, when, indignant at this, he, defendant, set out with his men and rode on a certain day, which he did not remember, from daybreak intending to attack the soldiery of the fortress of Paluau, seize them, and punish them if he could meet them, the said François, who rode among the others in the retinue of the said defendant, foretold from the start of this expedition that the defendant would not find on that day the said soldiery of the fortress of Paluau, and that in fact he did not meet them, so that the intention of the defendant was frustrated.

"Again, the same Gilles de Retz declared and confessed that he had detained in his power and caused to be killed two apprentices, one of Guillemain Sanxaye and the other of Petri Jaquet, named Princzay or Princé . . .

"Again, the said defendant declared and confessed in court that, at the time of his last stay at Vienne (*Veneti*) in the month of last July, Andrew Buschet handed over and delivered up to the said Gilles, defendant, in the dwelling house of a certain John Lemoyne at which the said Gilles, defendant, was at that time enjoying hospitality, a certain boy, . . . and that he himself afterwards caused the said Poitou to throw the killed lad into the privy of a residence belonging to a certain Boetdan, close by the residence of the said Lemoyne, in which residence or house of Boetdan the horses of said defendant had been sheltered (*apud marchiliam*) near the market-place of said Vienne, and that Poitou for this purpose flooded the privy so as to submerge and cover the corpse of said boy, lest it be discovered.

"Again, the said Gilles similarly declared and confessed that before the arrival of the aforesaid François he had had other conjurors of demons, that is to say, a certain trumpeter called de Mesnill, master John Ripparia, a certain Louis, master Anthony de Palermo, and another whose name he could not remember; that these conjurors at the instigation of said Gilles, defendant, made several incantations of spirits, at some of which the said Gilles, defendant, was present in person, both near the aforesaid Château de Machecoul and elsewhere [and that he attended], principally to see the circle or outline or sign of a circle drawn on the ground prior to the incantation, with the intention of seeing the devil, of speaking with him, and making bargains with him. But the same defendant declared that he never could see nor converse with the said devil, though for this purpose he had taken all the pains he could, so that indeed it was not the fault of the said defendant that he did not see the devil nor converse with him.

"Again, the frequently mentioned Gilles declared and confessed that the aforesaid de Mesnill, wizard, informed the defendant once that the devil, in order to do and fulfil the things which the said defendant intended to ask and obtain from the said devil, desired to receive from the said defendant a grant, written, made by him, defendant, with his own hand, and signed with the blood of one of his fingers, in which grant the aforesaid defendant should promise to give to the said devil whenever he appeared during the invocation of the said defendant, certain things which he, defendant, could not remember; and that the same defendant, for this purpose and end, signed the said grant with his own hand, with blood drawn from his little finger, and subjoined his own name to the said grant, i. e., *Gilles* [see p. 22]. That he could not accurately remember the other statements contained in this grant, except that he promised by the honour of said grant to deliver up to said devil the articles mentioned in the grant, provided that the devil would give or grant the same Gilles knowledge, power, and riches. But the defendant is quite certain, as he says, that whatsoever he may have promised the devil by this or other grants, he always and decidedly made exception of and reserved his soul and his life: and he says that this grant was not handed to the devil at this time, since he did not appear to the said Gilles, defendant, at or during said incantation.

"Furthermore, the said defendant likewise declared and confessed that once the said master John Ripparia made one of his invocations in a wood or grove situated near the Château de Pouzauges, and that this Ripparia, before going to make this invocation, armed himself with weapons and implements of protection to his body, and thus armed he approached the said grove intending to make the invocation;—and that, when the said defendant, accompanied by his servants and, especially, by Eustace, Henriet, and Stephen Corrillaud, *alias* Poitou, aforesaid, started after a little while towards the said grove and met the said de Ripparia returning from that grove, then the said de Ripparia told the said Gilles, defendant, that he had seen the devil coming to him in the guise of a leopard that passed in front of him and told something to him, de Ripparia, which, as he said, infused great fear into the said de Ripparia. And the defendant added in his narration, that the said de Ripparia, to whom the defendant had given the sum of twenty louis d'or (*regalium auri*), took his departure after this invocation, promising to return later to the said defendant, which he did not do.

"Similarly, the same accused said and confessed that when another invocation of the demons which the accused and a certain one of the above-mentioned invocators, whose name is not mentioned, and who was an associate of Gilles de la Sillé, made in a certain room of the above-mentioned Château Tiffauges, de la Sillé himself did not attempt to enter the circle or circular sign made in the said room for the invocation, nay, rather, he withdrew to a window of that room with the intention of jumping out if he should feel anything terrible approach, there holding in his arms an image of the Blessed Virgin Mary; and the said accused standing within the circular sign, feared very much, and especially as the said invocator forbade him to make the sign of the cross, as otherwise they, the accused and the invocator, would be in great danger, nor did the accused for this reason attempt to make that sign, but then remembering a certain prayer of the Blessed Virgin Mary which begins 'Alma,[4] said invocator ordered the said accused to go out of the circle, and withdrawing quickly and going out of the room, the invocator being left remaining there, and the door of the room being closed by the above-said invocator, he went to the aforesaid Gilles de la Sillé, who forthwith said to the accused that the invocator thus left in the room was beaten and struck to such an extent as if the striking was done by kicking. And when the accused heard this, he opened the room right away, and in the entrance of the room said accused saw said invocator [lying] on his face, grievously wounded and weakened in other parts of his body, among other strokes and blows then sustained by said invocator, . . . in the forehead and otherwise wounded so that the invocator could not support himself, wherefore said accused, fearing that said invocator by reason of that beating would die, wanted and made said invocator receive the sacrament of confession; he, however, did not die, but got well after that same trouncing.

"The said Gilles de Retz, accused, also said and confessed that he commissioned the aforesaid Gilles de la Sillé [to go] to the upper country to look for and bring to said Gilles, accused, invocators of demons or malignant spirits. And that this Gilles de

4   *Alma Redemptoris Mater*, an anthem chanted during Advent.

la Sillé, thus commissioned and then having returned, related to
the same Gilles, accused, how he, de Sillé, had found a woman
who occupied herself with such invocations, and that she said
to the same de Sillé that unless Gilles de Retz would remove his
heart from the Church and his chapel, he could never fulfil his
intention; and that the said de Sillé found in those parts another
woman who had said to the same de Sillé that unless the said
accused would desist and cease from a certain work on which
he was intent and which he desired to follow out, he would
never have a day's luck. Also, said de Sillé had found in these
parts an invocator whom the said de Sillé proposed and began,
as he said, to conduct to the said accused, but that on the way,
the invocator, being disposed to come to the said accused, as
he was crossing a river or stream, accidentally fell in. Also said
Gilles, accused, said and confessed that de Sillé brought another
invocator to said accused and that he died without delay; in and
from the obsequies of such unfortunate deceased and from other
previous difficulties, which interfering he could not come to the
aforesaid invocations and his other damnable intentions; he said
that he believed the Divine clemency and intercessory prayers
of the Church, from which his heart and hope never deviated,
mercifully preserved him from perishing in such risks and
dangers, and for this reason he proposed to desist from his bad
life for the future and to visit the [holy] places in Jerusalem and
to visit abroad the principal places of the life and Passion of his
Redeemer, and to perform other [penances] by which he might
mercifully obtain from his Redeemer the pardon of his sins.
Wherefore, after he had said and confessed freely and of his own
accord the aforesaid things at the trial, as recorded, he exhorted
the people there present, and especially the ecclesiastics who
were present in the majority, that they always hold in reverence
and in the highest esteem holy Mother Church and never depart
from it, especially adding that had he, the accused, not directed
and attached his heart and mind to the Church, he could never
have escaped the malice and schemes of the devil, nay, rather

he believed that the devil would long since have strangled him and almost have carried off his soul by reason of his enormous crimes and sins; and he, moreover, exhorted every head of a family to avoid permitting their children's being clothed in soft raiment and living in idleness, hinting and asserting that from idleness and excess at table many evils spring, more expressly declaring in his own case that idleness and the too frequent and too choice partaking of delicate meats and blood-stirring wines were the chief sources of his having committed so many sins and crimes.

"For which sins and crimes committed by him, as stated, he, Gilles de Retz, accused, humbly and in tears begged mercy and pardon of his Creator and Most Holy Redeemer, as well as of the parents and friends of the aforesaid children cruelly murdered, and of all others whom he had sinned against, or injured, both those there present or elsewhere, and the help of the devout prayers of all Christ's faithful and Christ's worshippers, both present and absent.

"Wherefore the aforesaid master, Guillermus Chapeillon, promoter in case of said Gilles de Retz, accused, having the free confession of the matter and the other facts legitimately proved against same accused, immediately asked that a certain day and suitable closing day of trial for same Gilles de Retz, accused, be preferred and assigned for bringing [trial] to an end, and seeing to its being brought to an end as well as for judgment and definite sentence [being pronounced] by said reverend Father in Christ, the Lord Bishop of Nantes, and Brother John Blouyn, vicar of said Inquisition, and by every one of them or of those, and by those assigned and deputed to this [trial], and made in writing and promulgated in [this] trial and trials of this kind: or that said Gilles de Retz, accused, should state cause, if he had a reasonable one, why this should not be done. Whereupon the lords, the Bishop, and the vicar of the aforesaid Inquisition said that Tuesday next was fixed, determined on, and assigned for the prosecutor and for Gilles de Retz, accused, he not opposing it, to proceed to justice, as it might seem necessary in this and similar trials.

"Of the aforesaid [things], said prosecutor asked that one and several documents be made and drawn up for him by us, the subscribed notaries and scribes. There were present in aforesaid place [of trial] reverend Father in Christ, Lord Jean Prigencii, Bishop of St. Brieuc, master Pierre de l'Hospital, President of Brittany, Robert de Ripparia and Lord Robert d'Espinay, aforesaid soldier, and the nobleman Yvone de Rocerff, as well as the honourable men, masters Yvon Coyer, dean, John Morelli, chanter, Graciano Ruitz, Guillermo Groygueti, licentiate of laws, Jean de Castrogironis, Peter Aprilis, Robert Vigerii, Gauffredo de Chevigneyo, licentiate of laws, the seigniors of Nantes, Gauffredo Piperarii, capicerio, Peter Hamonis, John Guerrine, John Vaedie, and John Symonis, the canons of the Church of the Blessed Mary of Nantes and St. Brieuc, Herveo Levy, Seneschal Corisopitensi, and master Guillermo de la Loherie, licentiate of laws, advocate of the secular court of Nantes, as well as several other witnesses gathered in [that] great crowd, being specially summoned and called for the aforesaid things.

(*Signed*)
"DE ALNETO. "
"JO. PARVI."
"G. LESNE."
"*Notaries*"

By this time all hope seemed to have departed from Gilles. He had none of the bravado that sustained him at the beginning of the trial. He apparently had recognised his condition and had thrown himself upon the mercy of God. One can easily understand how he was thus affected while under the influence of the saintly churchmen by whom he was surrounded, with their prayers and beseechings that if his body was to be condemned for the deeds done, he should at least save his soul from the fires of hell. When Gilles was interrogated before the court as to the genuineness of this confession, and asked if he desired to make any retraction or explanation, he seemed to add to, rather than detract from, it; and believing, as was probably the truth, that he could only save his soul by making a surrender of all his thoughts and a confession of all his sins, he seemed to insist on having the record of his crimes made fuller and in greater detail, so that none of them, even with all their horror, should be omitted. It was during this session that he used the remarkable words partially quoted in the early part of this book, page 7:

"If I have so much offended against God, I owe it, alas, to the evil direction that I received in my youth. I went, at that time, the reins upon my neck, free to pursue all my pleasures, and did not restrain myself from anything evil."

And addressing himself to the parents in the crowd, he said:

"O you, who have sons and daughters, I pray you to instruct them in good doctrine in their infancy and their youth, and to lead them with care in the paths of virtue."

The relief produced on his mind by his confession, casting off the great load he had been carrying, caused his spirits to rise to a contemplation of the situation, which produced a calm, if not a joy, in the assurance that he had made his peace with God and secured a place in Paradise. Apparently stimulated by this feeling, he grew eloquent, and though some of the words may have been put into his mouth by those who reported him, yet one can easily see that he was filled with emotion, and that the thoughts crowded thick upon him because of his belief that in this way his soul had escaped hell fire:

"Judged by the declaration that I have made here, of the faults of which I am culpable, by the shame which appears in my face, I hope to obtain more easily the Grace of God and the remission of my sins. I think they will be easier forgotten in His mercy. My entire youth was passed in the delicacies of the table, I was subject to my caprices, nothing to me was sacred, all the evils that I could do have been accomplished. In this I put all my hope, all my thought, all my care. Everything that was prohibited, everything that was dishonest, attracted me, and in order to obtain it there was no means, however shameful and disgraceful, that I was not ready to employ."

Addressing himself this time to the public present, he said:

"Fathers and mothers who hear me, and you all, friends, relatives, and guardians of the young whom you love, whoever you may be, I pray you be watchful over them, form for them good manners, set for them a good example, teach them healthy doctrine, nourish them in your hearts, but above all, do not fear to correct their faults, for, as I myself have been, so is it possible for them to become, and so likewise, they may fall into the same abyss."

As he sat down amidst the silence of that awful hour, a visible shudder ran over the audience; judges and priests, accustomed, one to condemn, the other to console, both hearing these terrible confessions of evil deeds, were visibly affected. Before any word or business could be spoken, Gilles arose again to say another word:

"Whatever may be the perils of my soul, I am still not drowned or lost—I am redeemable, and I believe that the clemencies of God and the suffrages of the holy Church, in which I have always put my hope and my heart, have succoured me with such mercy. To all who hear me, clerks and priests of the Church, I would say: love always our holy Mother Church, revere her, give to her always the greatest respect. If I had not had this reverence and respect for her in my heart and in my affliction, I never would have been able to escape the hands of the demon. The nature of my crimes is such, that without the protection of the Church, the demon would have strangled me and carried me, soul and body, to the depths."

It is reported that, addressing for a third time the fathers of families, he said:

"Guard you well, I pray you, to lift your infants above the delicacies of life and the fatal sweetness of idleness, for the excesses of appetite and the habits of idleness give rise to the greatest evils. Idleness, the delicacies of the table, the frequent use of wine, drinking, appetite, drunkenness, these things are the causes of my faults and my crimes. O God, my Creator and my well-beloved Redeemer, I ask mercy and pardon! And you, parents and friends of the infants that I have so cruelly put to death, you against whom I have sinned and whom I have so nearly destroyed, present or absent, in whatever place you may be, as Christians and faithfuls of Jesus Christ, I pray you on my knees and with tears, to accord to me, oh, to give to me, the succour and aid of your pious prayers."

The effect of these words can be better understood than described. Amid the impressive silence of such a spectacle, nothing was to be said. The court adjourned until the next day, Tuesday, October 25th, and the crowd poured silently and sorrowfully into the streets on their way to their homes, each heart filled with the most profound emotions, and each person cherishing the remembrance of the most solemn scene he had ever witnessed and the gravest advice he had ever heard.

The session of the next day was to hear the sentence of the court. It had been reduced to writing, and was read by the clerk, Jacques Pencoetdic, an official of the church of Nantes:

"In the holy name of Christ, we, Jean, Bishop of Nantes, and

Brother Jean Blouyn, Bachelor of Holy Scripture of the order of Friars Preachers and the Delegate for the Inquisitor for heresy for the city and diocese of Nantes, in session as attributed, and having nothing before our eyes but God alone, the advice and consent of our Lord Bishop, the Jurisconsuls, the doctors, professors of Holy Scripture here present; after having examined all the depositions of the witnesses in charge called in our own name and in the name of the prosecutor deputised by us, against Gilles de Retz, our subject, and under our jurisdiction, after having reduced to writing and digested the depositions, after having heard his own proper confession made spontaneously in our presence, and after having weighed and considered these and all other reasons which can affect our determination, we pronounce, we decide, we declare, that thou, Gilles de Retz, cited before our tribunal, art shamefully culpable of heresy, apostacy, invocation of demons; that for these crimes, thou hast incurred the sentence of excommunication and all the other punishments determined by right and by law; and, finally, thou oughtest to be punished and corrected according to the will of the law and the exigencies of the holy canons, as an heretic, apostate, and invocator of demons."

The second sentence was in similar language, concluding, however, as follows:

"Thou, Gilles de Retz, hast shamefully committed crimes with infants of one or the other sex; thou hast committed sacrilege; hast violated the immunities of the Church; by these crimes, thou hast incurred the sentence of excommunication and all other punishments fixed by law; and thou art, by consequence, to be punished and corrected according to thy salvation and the will and exigencies of law and the holy canons."

All Gilles's fears returned when he realised that he was to be convicted of heresy and condemned to excommunication.

Falling on his knees, tears in his eyes, trembling, he humbly pleaded and begged the judges to lift from his life, now so near ended and so worthless, this excommunication. After consultation together, it was determined by the Bishop and the Vice-Inquisitor to grant this prayer, and the decree of excommunication was annulled in the usual form. Gilles was admitted to the administration of the Holy Sacraments, and permission given him to commune with the faithful. Gilles immediately demanded the appointment of a priest to hear him in confession, that he might profess his penitence and receive absolution from his sins, and the Frère Jean Juvenal, a Carmelite of Plouarmel, was designated for that purpose.

So terminated the ecclesiastical trial of Gilles de Retz. It commenced on the 17th of September and lasted one month and eight days. It ended in his conviction of the only crimes of which the ecclesiastical court had jurisdiction, to wit, heresy, apostacy, and invocation of demons. The sentence was excommunication, which, we have seen, was lifted, and the final outcome of this trial was the repentance of Gilles de Retz.

Now we turn to the process instituted by the civil tribunal for the trial of Gilles upon other charges than those of which he was convicted by the ecclesiastical court. The usual close of the sentence of an ecclesiastical court, wherein the accused was charged with other crimes than those with which the court had jurisdiction, would be: "Go in peace, the Church can no longer defend thee, she delivers thee to the secular arm" (*bras séculier*). But this declaration was not made; it was useless, for it was well known to the judges that the civil court had already been organised and had taken cognisance and jurisdiction of the various crimes of Gilles, such as had been charged and so well proved before the ecclesiastical court.

CHAPTER VI

THE TRIAL BEFORE THE CIVIL COURT

UPON the arrest of Gilles and his henchmen, and during their trial before the ecclesiastical court, the army of retainers which had been employed by him, including his chapel and all his familiars, fled as would a flock of young chickens on the approach of a hawk. François Prelati, Eustache Blanchet, Henriet Griard, and Poitou seem to have been all who were arrested with Gilles. Gilles de Sillé and Roger de Briqueville had fled to the south before the blow fell. The rest got under cover as quickly as possible; instead of standing by their master, they got as far away from him as they could. Gilles was the only one tried by the ecclesiastical tribunal. No particular reason has been given why François and Blanchet were not tried with him, for they were undoubtedly guilty, equally with Gilles, of the charges of sorcery and invocation of demons; but they were priests, one of them an Italian priest, and whether they were promised freedom in consideration of their testimony against Gilles, is now unknown.

When, on the 19th of October, it had been decided by the ecclesiastical court to apply the torture to Gilles, it was done on the confessions of his accomplices. Why François Prelati and Eustache Blanchet had been excused or overlooked is, as has been said, unknown; but Henriet Griard and Poitou were then delivered to the civil court for trial. This civil court was presided over by Pierre de l'Hospital, who, as has been seen, had assisted in the ecclesiastical court, and was necessarily officially cognisant of the developments. Pierre de l'Hospital was the chief justice of the duchy of Brittany, and the civil courts were under

126

his authority; so immediately after the confessions of Henriet and Poitou, they were transferred to the civil authorities, and Pierre de l'Hospital, as supreme judge, brought them before the court on the 20th or 21st of October. The civil court held its session at the Bouffay, then, and until 1848, the *Palais de Justice*. The Bouffay had been a castle, but had been reconstructed and used as the *Palais de Justice* during many centuries. It was in proximity to the Château de Nantes. It was enclosed in a high wall, possibly to make a jail-yard, and occupied the present Place, or Market, Bouffay.

It was within this palace yard that the celebrated trial by duel took place, by direction or authority of the Duke of Brittany, between Count Robert Beaumanoir and Sieur Pierre Tournemine, on a charge of murder made by the former against the latter.

The castle, or palace, has been destroyed, as well as the wall, and it now stands all open. One side of the Place abuts on the river Loire, adjoining the Bridge de la Poissonerie, over which the prisoners were taken to the Prairie Madeleine, the place of execution.

The proceedings of the civil court need not be followed in their details. Preparing for the trial, as is the custom of criminal courts in France, the prosecutor called the witnesses before him, and took down their depositions, and it is worth our while to pause and examine the record as it appears in the archives of the department of Loire-Inférieure.

The records of the two trials, the ecclesiastical and the civil, on file in the Departmental Archives, are unequal in the extent and detail with which they have been respectively reported. It is to be explained that it is a considerable work, and scarcely possible to have been completed in all its parts as the trial progressed, without immense labour on the part of the clerks and notaries. The proceedings of the ecclesiastical court, reported in Latin, comprise three hundred and eight pages, of which the photograph on page 137 of this memoir is a sample.

The proceedings of the civil court, in French, comprise a hundred and nine pages, the two together making four hundred and twenty pages in parchment, without including the sentence, which was in Latin, much mixed with French. The sentence is about the size of the original Declaration of Independence of the United States. It is said to have been written in its entirety in a single night, and an inspection of it corroborates the story, for it bears evidence, by way of erasures and interlineations, of haste and rapid work.

The report of the evidence in the ecclesiastical trial is not nearly so satisfactory, nor has it been recorded so clearly, or with so much detail, as was that in the civil court. It is also much more convenient to render that of the civil trial, and the author has, therefore, used it in making a transcript. (Appendix D.)

It must not be forgotten that the evidence was taken by deposition, out of court; that it was rendered, not in the language of the witness, but of the scribe. The depositions were not signed by the witnesses, but were reported to the court under the signature of the notary or commissioner. Eighty-six witnesses were examined, and their testimony appears to have been reduced to writing by Jean Colin, and certified to by Jean de Touscheronde. The dates of the various sessions are not given, but each witness, or each batch of witnesses, appears to have been examined independently and certified to separately. This examination of witnesses in the civil court seems to have begun about as early as did that in the ecclesiastical trial, for the first record is under date of September 18, 1440. For the purpose of showing the style of the French language in use at that time, that it may be compared with modern French, and the changes noted, the heading of these depositions is here reproduced textually:

"*September* 18, 1440.

"Informacion et enqueste a trouver, se estre peut, que le
sire de Rais, ses gens et complices, out prins et fait prandre
pluseurs petiz enffans et autres gens, et les murtriz et occiis pour
en avoir le sang, le cueur, le faye et autres parties d'elx, pour
en faire sacrifice au deable, et autres malefices, de quoy il est
grant clamour. Celle enqueste faite par Jehan de Touscheronde,
commissaire de duc, nostre souverain seigneur, en ceste matere,
appellé Jehan Colin, pour le prouchain tesmoign que eust en sa
compaignie, le xviiie jour de septembre, l'an mil IIII C quarante."

Before reporting the testimony in the depositions against
Gilles de Retz, and that it may be better understood, it should be
explained that there were two methods pursued by Gilles in the
abduction of children: one, the secret and forcible abduction,
and the other the hiring of the child for service as a page, or
his being taken with the consent of the parents on a pretended
duty, by which he should be attached to the retinue of the Baron.
Both systems were pursued, and, it is believed, always by the
followers and "familiars" of the Baron, for it does not appear
that he was ever personally engaged in either. The demand of
the parent for the presence of the child was always put off by
indefinite statements: the boy was at another château, or he had
gone with the masters, or men-at-arms, and would be absent
for an indefinite time; sometimes, that he had gone to a distant
province; other times, that he had fled and was a fugitive,
and they knew not his whereabouts. These were all equivocal
responses, and far from satisfactory to the demanders; but out of
them there grew the reports circulated through the country, as
set forth in the first pages of Chapter IV.

On the trial, Henriet Griart and Poitou made no defence, but
pleaded guilty. They confessed openly their crime, and being
pushed to detail, they admitted that they had been concerned
in the abduction of more than fifty children, and Henriet added

that during his last trip to Jocelyn with Gilles de Retz, he had captured three of them with his own hands.

The confession of Henriet and of Corrillaud called Poitou, appears in the records, and following it, on October 23d, is the condemnation by the civil court under Pierre de l'Hospital, as follows:

"After the confession of the aforesaid Henriet and Poitou, and on the advice of the assistants, advocates and others, heard in the case, and considering all the facts, it was adjudged and declared by the aforesaid seignior the President, that the aforesaid Henriet and Poitou should, and ought to be, hung and burned" (*penduz et ars*).

But the execution of the sentence was postponed to await the conclusion of the trial of Gilles before the ecclesiastical court.

On the 25th of October, Gilles's sentence was passed upon him by the ecclesiastical court, and he was turned over to the civil court (*bras séculeir*). He was delivered to the prison at the Bouffay on the same evening, and the next morning was brought before the civil court with Pierre de l'Hospital as supreme judge. All hope of escape was lost to Gilles, and, like his accomplices, he seemed to be more interested for the salvation of his soul than care for his body. He made no defence,—indeed defence was useless, for the trial was only a formality. Being charged with the crime of murder and interrogated as to the facts, he repeated his confession of guilt.

In the consultation of the court as to the sentence, there were some differences of opinion among the judges. That he merited death, there was no question, and that appears to have been accepted by all. But as to the manner of death and the degree of odium to be attached thereto, there was some debate. However, as he had been excommunicated by the Church, as his accomplices had already been sentenced *penduz et ars*, and as the crime shocked all the world who knew of it, the argument prevailed that, as Gilles had been the chief promoter, and as he and his two accomplices had been together in their crimes they should not be separated in their punishments, and therefore first, a fine should be upon him of fifty thousand pounds; and second, that he should be hung and burned alive on the gibbet of Piesse.

Piesse was a little open prairie on the island of La Madeleine in the river opposite, forming part of the city of Nantes. It was reached by two bridges communicating with the Place Bouffay.

Pierre de l'Hospital in pronouncing the sentence upon Gilles, concluded:

> "You have naught to rely upon now but the mercy of God; I ask you so to dispose yourself as to die in good state, and to seek repentance for having committed such great crimes. To-morrow, at one o'clock, the sentence against you will be carried into effect."

Gilles preferred three petitions, through the judge, to the Bishop. One, that the execution of the three, himself and his two servants, should be at one and the same time, to the end that he might comfort and aid them by his presence upon that dread occasion; that they should see that his execution actually took place, and should not be tormented with the thought that either his wealth or power could procure the postponement of the execution, and finally, or possibly, a pardon. The second was, that his ashes might be buried in consecrated ground; and when this prayer was granted, he chose the Carmelite church at Nantes. The third was, that on the day of the execution, a procession of litany, such as was common in that country, should be organised to make prayers to God for him and his two servants, that they might be sustained and supported in their repentance, and that their salvation might be assured. Accordingly, on the morrow, at nine o'clock, this procession was organised and marched through the streets of the city in the most solemn manner, headed by the clergy of all ranks, reciting the prayers for the dead.

CHAPTER VII

THE EXECUTION

ON October 26, 1440, at eleven o'clock, the time fixed, the procession approached the prison Bouffay; Gilles, Henriet, and Poitou were brought out, and with this long procession for an escort, were conducted across the two bridges to the place of execution. The two courts, ecclesiastical and civil, were present, and it has been said that the Duke of Brittany was also present. Three gibbets had been erected with their cross-arms, and at the foot of each a pile of wood and fagots (*bucher*) was laid. It is needless to describe the details of the execution. Some of them may be apocryphal; they were not recorded at the time, and they may have been made for the occasion; in any event, they add nothing to the strength of the story. It seems agreed, however, that at the given signal the three malefactors were suspended by ropes from the gibbets, that the wood was fired, and that they were hung and burned at the same time; that they died with words of repentance upon their lips, expressions of hope for pardon from the God whom they had offended, and stating their hopes and beliefs of salvation. There was no sermon, no reading of sentences, no prolongation of agony. Prayers for the dead were continually recited, but the execution proceeded with as much rapidity as possible.

The historians of the day, Monstrelet, Chartier, Argentré, all agree that the body of Gilles was rescued from the flames before it was burned to ashes, and enclosed in a coffin and carried to the church of the Carmelites at Nantes, where it was buried privately and without ceremony, while the ashes of the two accomplices were scattered to the winds of heaven and the waves of the Loire.

Grotto of Bonne Vierge de Crée-Lait.
Expiatory altar of Gilles, erected by his daughter.

This was the punishment of Gilles de Retz, and this the expiation of his crimes. It is curious to remark its effect on human nature, and how it was regarded by the people. If Gilles de Retz had escaped the punishment of his crimes, the whole country would have been in arms, and he would have been denounced in the fiercest terms, as the most execrable of human beings. But, after having suffered this terrible punishment before the eyes of all men, and it was thus made known throughout the country, the spirit of hate and vengeance seems to have turned to pity, and sorrow and grief seem to have taken their places.

In commemoration of his sufferings, an altar was erected in his memory and to his name, upon the spot where he died. A niche was made for the reception of a statue, though none appears to have been erected, and, unexplainable as it is,—almost marvellous,—it came in after years to be called the altar of the "Bonne Vierge de Créé-Lait." The spot where was executed this man, who had decimated Brittany by the abduction and murder of its infants, came in a superstitious manner to be esteemed as a place of value in furnishing milk for nursing mothers. Offerings of flowers and similar objects were frequently placed upon the altar to secure the good offices of Saint Anne, who was supposed to have it in charge. This is evidence, not only of the instability of the judgment of the multitude and the changeableness of the public, but the elusiveness of and want of dependence in tradition.

The family of Gilles seem to have made no demonstration, not even an appearance, during this trying time. No record or mention is made of their presence at the trial, or of any interest therein. His widow married within the year, and his daughter Marie, then about fifteen years of age, married within two years, after his death. His widow married Jean de Vendôme, and the daughter's first husband was Prégent de Coétivy, Admiral of France. These united in a *Mémoire* addressed to the King of France, to save the property that had belonged to Gilles de Retz from confiscation by the Duke of Brittany. Prégent de Coétivy was killed on June 20, 1450, during the siege of Cherbourg, by a cannon-shot. His widow (Gilles's daughter) married, for a second husband, André de Laval, her cousin. She died, without issue, November 1, 1457, and was buried in the Church of Notre Dame, at Vitré. René de la Suze, brother of Gilles, married Anne de Champagne. He left a daughter, Jeanne de Retz, who married François de Chauvigny, the Prince of Deol, April 11, 1446. They had one child, a son, André de Chauvigny, who died, unmarried, in 1502. And thus, within sixty-two years after the death of Gilles de Retz, his family became extinct.

APPENDIX A

MOTHER GOOSE PUBLICATIONS

Nearly every publisher in France, and many of those in England and the United States, have issued editions of Mother Goose stories. Most of those from France have been reprints, with variation, of the originals by Perrault: Boussod; B. Bernardin; Biblioth. Nat.; MM. Chavery; Dentu; Flammarion; Boulanger; Lemerre; Bornemann; Cattier; Duployé; Fayard; E. Guérin; Hachette; G. Delarue; Garnier Frères; Magnin.

The editions of Mother Goose fairy tales and nursery rhymes in England and the United States are given in the publishers' catalogues with essays on the same subject as follows:

MOTHER GOOSE:

The Original Mother Goose's Melodies as First Issued about 1760. W. H. Whitmore. 1890. Munsell.
—— *Fairy Tales of Mother Goose*, first collected by Perrault, 1696. 1892. Damrell.
Favourite Rhymes from Mother Goose. Maud Humphrey. 1891–1893. Stokes.
Nursery Rhymes, Tales, and Jingles. 1890. Routledge.
Contes des fées, with notes and vocabulary. 1884. Macmillan.
Fairy Tales. 1877–1882. Routledge.
Tales from Perrault, translated by J. R. Planche, 1860. 1891. Routledge.
Mother Goose, or the Old Nursery Rhymes. Illustrated by K. Greenaway, 1881. Routledge.

Mother Goose Goslings. E. W. Talbot. Cassell, P., G. & Co.
Mother Goose Rhymes, with silhouette illustrations
    by J. F. Goodrich, 1877. 1879. Lee & Shepard.
Mother Goose Masquerades. Mrs. E. D.
    Kendall. Lee & Shepard.
Mother Goose Melodies. Illustrated. 1879. Lippincott.
Mother Goose Melodies, with Chimes, Rhymes,
    and Jingles, with pictures designed by Billings
    and engraved by Hartwell. 1878.
Mother Goose Set to Music. New edition.
    Illustrated. 8°. 1877. McLoughlin.
Mother Goose Fairy Tales, illustrated by eminent
    artists. 1877. New edition, 1882. Routledge.
Mother Goose Melodies, or Songs for the Nursery. Illustrated
    in color by A. Kappes. 1879. Houghton, Osgood & Co.
Mother Goose's Nursery Rhymes. Collection of
    alphabets, rhymes, tales, and jingles. Illustrated.
    1876. New edition, 1882. Routledge.
Mother Goose's Nursery Rhymes.
    Illustrated. 1877. McLoughlin.
Mother Goose's Nursery Rhymes and Fairy
    Tales. Illustrated. 1877. Routledge.
Nursery Rhymes and Fairy Tales. 1891. Routledge.
Nursery Rhymes and Fairy Tales. 1892–1896. Nister.
"Mother Goose's Melodies." Joel Benton. New
    York *Times, Saturday Review,* Feb. 5, 1899.
"Who Was Mother Goose?" Thomas Wilson. *St. Nicholas.*

An investigation of the foregoing volumes will show a series of Mother Goose stories other than those written by Perrault. These are well-known rhymes and jingles principally from England, and are of indefinite and undetermined age.

The edition above mentioned by W. H. Whitmore, gives its history of the English and American Mother Goose. The collection was first made for and by John Newbery of London, about A.D. 1760. Its popularity was due to the Boston editions of Monroe & Francis, A.D. 1824–1860.

The first rhyme in these editions was styled "A Love Song":

> "There was a little man,
>   Who wooed a little maid;
> And he said, 'Little maid,
>   Will you wed, wed, wed?'"

Mr. Whitmore examines the claim made for the first time in 1856 that the origin of these melodies was due to Mrs. Elizabeth Goose, or Vergoose, of Boston, and that her son-in-law, Thomas Fleet, published a volume containing them in 1719, and pronounces the claim without foundation.

APPENDIX B

BLUEBEARD STORIES

The story of Bluebeard has permeated modern literature. Reference is made to some of its publications.

It appeared as a comedy with three acts, under the name of *Barbe-Bleue*. The music was by Grétry, and it was presented for the first time at Paris in the Théâtre des Italiens in 1789.

Another was an opera bouffe written by MM. Henry Meilhac and Ludovic Halévy, music by Offenbach, presented for the first time at Paris in the Théâtre des Variétés in 1866.

Monsieur Charles Lemire published, in 1894, a lyric representation with music, dances, etc., in four parts and ten scenes, entitled *Barbe-Bleue* (Le sire de Rais). Some of the scenes represented the interior of the Hôtel de la Suze, the public square at Nantes, the Château de Tiffauges, the gate of Machecoul (the arrest), Château de Nantes (the trial), Prairie Piesse (the execution), ending with an allegoric apotheosis.

A Picardy romance of Comte Ory was rendered by Scribe and Rossini into an opera in which the characteristics of Gilles de Retz were presented in the hero.

Walkenaer has investigated, with marvellous patience, the tradition of Bluebeard, and has sought to trace it throughout its various ramifications in literature.

La Rousse in his *Great French Dictionary of the XIXth Century*, under the title of *Barbe-Bleue*, introduces quotations from French littérateurs who have referred to Bluebeard: J. Sandeau, Toussenel, H. de Balzac, Ch. Nadar, Max. du Camp, Oct. Feuillet.

Essays or volumes on Bluebeard have appeared either separately or in magazines or newspapers as shown in the following list:

"Bluebeard." E. Vizelly. *Gentlemen's*
    Magazine, N. S., vol. xxii., p. 368.
—— T. C. Woolsey. *Lakeside*, vol. v., p. 314.
—— Origin of Story of. W. C. Taylor.
    Bentley, vol. xxiii., p. 136.
—— Original. *Once a Week*, vol. xviii., p. 15.
—— Rehabilitated, Verses. W. H. Harrison.
    Dub. Univ., vol. xc, p. 728.
"Bluebeard's Ghost." W. M. Thackeray.
    Fraser, vol. xxviii., p. 413.
"Bluebeard's Keys." *Cornn.*, vol. xxiii., pp. 192, 688. Same
    article *Living Age*, vol. cviii., p. 685; vol. cx., p. 139.
"Bluebeard." H. C. Lea. *Nation*, vol. xliii., p. 377.
"Gilles de Retz, Baron de: Original Bluebeard."
    L. Frechette. *Arena*, vol. i., p. 141.
"Bluebeard, Case of." P. Edwards. *Green Bag*, vol. v., p. 543D.
"Maréchal de Retz." *Belgra*, vol. lxxx., p. 58.
Gilles de Retz (Barbe-Bleue). L'Abbé Eugene
    Bossard. 1886. H. Champion.
Barbe-Bleue, de la Légende et de l'Histoire.
    Ch. Lemire. 1886. Ernest Leroux.

The works of Abbé Bossard and M. Charles Lemire have been issued since the author left Nantes. Much of the matter in this paper was prepared before these volumes were issued. But the author has not scrupled to use them, as he has those of Michelet, Monstrelet, or Guépin, or to verify from them what he has written, especially their later rendition of the archives. He had access to these records equally with these gentlemen, but he freely acknowledges the aid received from the printed copy of ancient manuscripts, the difficulties of which will be apparent on an examination of the photographic copy on page 137.

M. Paul Saunière published in the *Publicité* at Nantes, a feuilleton entitled *Barbe-Bleue*, and a novel entitled *The Black Douglas*, by S. R. Crockett, lately published, and a book entitled *La Bas*, by Huysmanns, all deal with Gilles de Retz.

APPENDIX C

MYSTERY OF THE SIEGE OF ORLEANS

Abbé Bossard is authority for the statement that the unique and original manuscript of the *Mystery of Orleans* in modern times is in the library of the Vatican, No. 1022, registered under *de la reine de Suède* (Queen of Sweden). This copy came from the library de Fleury or of Saint-Henoit-sur-Loire. It was written, he says, in the second half of the sixteenth century, and made a quarto volume of 509 leaves with 20,529 lines, and its author is unknown.

It was published for the first time (from the manuscript in the Vatican library in 1862), by MM. Guessard et de Certain, and forms part of the great collection of *documents inédits de l'histoire de France*. Quicherat says that the first author in modern times to mention the *Mystery of the Siege of Orleans* was M. Paul Lacroix in his *Dissertation sur quelques points curieux de l'histoire de France* (Paris, 1839). M. Adelbert Keller in his *Ronvart* (Mannheim, 1844), gave a more extended notice with extracts. M. Salmon, a student in the *École des Chartes*, made elaborate notes of the Vatican MSS., which notes fell into the hands of M. Quicherat while writing his *Procès de condemnation et réhabilitation de Jeanne d'Arc*.

Extracts from the
"Mystery of the Siege of Orleans"
as acted by Gilles de Retz

According to this drama, it was Gilles de Retz, with Ambroise de Loré, who were charged by the king to conduct and act as guards for Joan of Arc from Blois to Orleans.

There is in the drama or poem the following speech made by the King to the Maid, directing her to go to Orleans:

> "Et pour vous conduire voz gens
> Aurez le maréchal de Rais,
> Et ung gentilhomme vaillant
> Ambroise de Loré arés;
> Esquelz je commande exprès
> Ou il vous plaisa vous conduisent,
> En quelque lieu, soit loing, soit près."

The Marshal de Retz says to the Maid:

> "Dame, que vous plaist il de faire?
> Nous sommes au plus près de Blois;
> Se vous y voulez point retraire
> Et reposer deux jours ou trois,
> Pour savoir où sont les Anglois,
> Aussi pour rafrachir vos gens,
> Ou se vous aymez mieulx ainçois
> Aller droict jusques à Orléans?"

To which the Maid responded:

> "Monseigneur, je suis bien contans
> Que à Blois donques nous allons,
> Pour noz gens la contre atmendans;
> Ce pendant, aussi penserons

146

De noz affaires, et manderons
Es Anglais que devant Orléans
S'en voisent, ou combatuz seront,
En mon Dieu, de moy et mes gens."

The Marshal to the Maid:

"Madame, tout incontinant,
Vostre vouloir acomplirons;
Nous ferons assembler noz gens,
Et presentement partirons.
Droit à Orleans, nous nous menrons,
Dame Jehanne, sans plus atendre."

The Maid responded:

"Je vous empry, faictes le dont,
Et vous pry y vueillez entendre."

A discussion took place as to the proper route to follow. The
Marshal thus expressed himself:

"Je doute aller par la Beausse:
Le plus fort des Anglois y est,
Toute leur puissance et force,
Et tout le pays à eulx est.
Y nous pourroient donner arrest,
S'i savoyent nostre venue,
Et peut estre grant intérest
Seroit a nostre survenue.
Si me semble que vauldroit mieulx
Y aller devers la Sauloigne:
Le dangier n'est pas si perilleux
Et n'y a pas fort grant esloigne.
Mieulx vault faire nostre besoigne,

147

Et le dangier passer ainsi,
Entret par la porte Bourgoigne,
Et yrons passer à Checy."

Ambroise de Loré responds:

"Vous avez très bien devisé,
A Checy, nous y fault aller;
Et est a vous bien advisé:
Vous ne pourriez mieulx conseiller.
Si n'en conviendra point parler
A la Pucelle nullement;
Si non que on la veult mener
Droit à Orleans, tant seullement."

This resolution being taken, Jean de Metz asked if it was not time to notify the Maid; to whom Gilles expressed his readiness to depart instantly:

"Je suis prest aussi, par mon âme,
A aller quant elle vouldra.
Dame, se il vous plaist partir.
Voicy en point trestouz vos gens,
Pour vostre vouloir accomplir
A vous convoyer à Orléans."

The Maid responded:

"En mon Dieu, croy que il est tant
Et avons beaucoup demeuré,
Que, ainsi comme je l'entend,
Orléans a beaucoup enduré."

The Marshal to the Maid on their arrival at Checy:

"Dame Jehanne, la Dieu mercy,
Vous estes bien icy venue,
En ceste ville de Checy,
Sans nulle fortune avoir eue.
Vous n'estes pas que à une lieue
D'Orléans, comme je puis entendre;
Ferons icy une repeue,
Puis à Orléans yrons descendre."

The English are put to flight; the Maid, about to return to the
King, says to her companions in arms:

"Si est le baron de Colonnes,
Viendra avecq moy, si luy plaist.
De par moy luy prie et denonces
Que luy et ses gens soient prest,
Avecques le sire de Rais,
Se c'est son plaisir y venir.
Je les en supplie par exprest
Compaignie me veullent tenir."

The Sire of Colonnes accepts the invitation, as does the Baron
de Retz, who says:

"Aussi moy, dame, ne doubtez.
Faire vueil ce qui vous plaira;
Mes aliez et depputez,
Dame, sachez, tout y vendra.
Et vostre voloir on fera
Du tout en tout, à vostre guise,
Et quand vouldrez on partira,
En faisant à vostre devise."

The Maid to both:

149

"Mes bons seigneurs, je vous mercie,
Tant comme faire je le puis,
De vostre haulte courtoisie.
Nobles, vaillans princes gentilz
Quant ainsi vous estes soubmis
A mes bons voloirs acomplir.
Je vous en rens cinq cens mercis
Qu'i vous plaist cest honneur m'offrir."

APPENDIX D

DEPOSITIONS AGAINST GILLES

Peronne Loessart of Rochebernart, makes oath that the Baron de Retz, on returning from Vannes with his retinue, stopped in her town, at the Hotel of Jean Colin, in the immediate neighbourhood of her house. She had a son ten years of age then going to school whom one of the retinue of Gilles, called Poitou, desired to obtain as his page. It was agreed that he should have four pounds (*livres*) for his services, and Peronne, *cent souls* (*sous*), five francs, for a dress, and Poitou should continue the boy at school.

A pony was bought from the hotel-keeper for the boy to ride, and he departed on the morrow in the company. She talked with Gilles de Retz, and he commended her wisdom in placing the boy, and assured her it would be for her and his advantage. She had never seen her son afterwards, though this had taken place two years before. On a future journey, she had met the servants of Gilles, and on demanding news of her son, was informed that he was either at Tiffauges or Pouzauges.

(*Signed*)
DE TOUSCHERONDE.[5]

Jean Colin, his wife Olive, and her mother, support Peronne, and Colin says that he sold Poitou a pony for the sum of LX s.,

---

5   The depositions were all signed by Touscheronde and some other.

on which the boy was mounted and departed with the rest of the company.

Jean le Meignen, his wife, Allain Dulis, Perrot Dupouez, Guillaume Ganton, Guillaume Portuys, Jean le Fevre, clerc, all of Saint Étienne de Montluc (Loire-Inférieure) depose on their oaths that since about three years ago they had known a Guillaume Brice of their parish. He was a mendicant and had a son about eight or nine years of age named Jamet; that the father was now dead about one year; that last Saint John's day the said child disappeared and had never been heard of since in the neighbourhood. No one knew what had become of him. He was last seen near the wood of Saint Étienne, and Dupouez says that about the same time he met a woman of fifty or sixty years, hardened and strong, with a visage *vermaillé* (bronzed), supposed to be *la Meffraye*, who, it was believed, had abducted the boy. She was making her way towards Nantes.

Guillaume Fouraige, his wife Jehanne, the wife of Jean le Flou, Richarde, wife of Jean Gaudeau, from the Port de Launay near Coueron (Loire-Inférieure), record on their oaths the loss of the son, an infant of about twelve years, of Jean Bernart, their neighbour; that he started in the direction of Machecoul to ask alms (on a begging expedition) from which he had never returned, nor had anybody in their neighbourhood ever received news of him. The woman, Fouraige, told of meeting or seeing an old woman with a gray gown and black bonnet (supposed to be *Meffraye*) with a young boy in her company, who said she was on her way to Machecoul. In two or three days she returned alone. Being asked what had become of the child, she responded that she had placed him to live with a good master.

28, 29, and 30 September, 1440.

André Barbe, shoemaker, living at Machecoul, says that since Easter he has heard that the son of Georget le Barbier has been lost; that he (the witness) had seen the boy on a certain day gathering apples in the rear of the hotel Rondeau, and since that time he had never been seen in the neighbourhood; that the mothers of the neighbourhood had great fear for the loss of their children and guarded them very closely. He had been at Saint Jean d'Angely where some of the residents demanded whence he came, and when he said "from Machecoul," they responded, "That is the place where they eat the small children." He recounts the loss of several other children from his neighbourhood: Guillaume Jeudon, Jehannot Roucin, Alexandre Chastelier. He had heard at the church of Trinity de Machecoul, a stranger in search of his child of seven years, who had been gone for eight months or more.

Jehannet, wife of Guillaume Sergent, of Saint Croix de Machecoul, said that during the Pentecost a year before, she and her husband went to dig the field to sow hemp, leaving in their house a son of eight years to care for a baby one and a-half years. On their return the boy was gone and has never been heard of seen since.

Georget le Barbier, living near the gates of the Château de Machecoul, deposed that he had a son named Guillaume, of the age of eighteen years, that about the fête of Saint Barnabas he went after dinner to Machecoul to play *pelote*; that since vespers of the day on which he had played *pelote* he had never been seen or heard of, although he, the father, had made every investigation and demand possible. He further says it is notorious and the people murmur, saying that infants are murdered in the said château. He has also heard that the boy who was page of Monsieur François Prelati, and who lived with him, was also lost.

Guillaume Hylairet, and his wife Jehanne, living at Machecoul, have heard say that the son of the said Georget le Barbier had been lost, and no one knew where he was or what had become of him. They say, further, that about eight or seven years ago they had living with them a child of twelve years, the son of Jean Jeudon, as an apprentice to learn the trade of furrier;

that Gilles de Sillé, accompanied by Roger de Briqueville, had asked to send the boy to the château of Machecoul with a message, which was accordingly done; that the boy never returned and was never seen or heard of in the neighbourhood; that upon his demand, made to Sillé and Briqueville, as to what had become of the boy, they responded that he was possibly at Tiffauges, but thought some of the *larrons* (thieves) had carried him off to be their page; that he, the witness, knew of the loss of the infants of Jehannet Roucin and Alexandre Chastelier; that he had heard the parents complain of their loss *doloreusement*. Guillaume says that about five years since he heard a man, Jean du Jardin, then living with Monsieur Roger de Briqueville, say that they had found at the castle of Champtocé a caskful, *toute plaine*, of the bodies of dead infants; that it was common and notorious talk that these infants were murdered at the château of Machecoul; that he has heard the same complaint made by others, of the *perdicion d'autres enffants*.

Jehan Thipholoz, Sr., Jehan Thifoloz, Jr., Jouhan Aubin, Clemens Doré, of Tonaye (Charente-Inférieure) have heard the complaints of Mathelin Thouars, of the same parish, for about half a year, that his son, a child about twelve years, had been lost, and that he had no knowledge of his whereabouts, nor could he obtain any news of him.

Jehan Roucin, of Machecoul, says that about nine years ago his son, a child then about nine years of age, was in the field guarding the cattle; at night he did not return, and has never returned, nor have they ever had any news of him. They were told by a neighbour, since dead, that she had seen Gilles de Sillé with a tabart and an estamine (a sort of cloak and veil) going to and speaking with the child, whom he conducted to the postern-gate of the château; that the complaints of their neighbours, especially Jeudon, of the loss of their infants, are notorious.

Johanne, widow of Hemery Edelin, and previous wife of Jehan Bonneau, of Machecoul, says that she had a son of the age of eight years, going to school; that he lived with his grandmother near the château. About eight years ago her child was lost and has never been heard of since; that she knew the boy Roucin, and another of Geudon, which were lost; that about fifteen days after, another child, that of Macé Sorin, was also lost; that this created a great clamour, upon which it was explained that these children, with others, had been captured to serve as hostages with the English, for the deliverance of Monsieur Michel de Sillé, then prisoner, and it was said that the ransom of the said Michel had been fixed by the English at twenty-four male infants. About two or three years before, the witness had seen, at Machecoul, a stranger from Saint Mesme, near Chinon, who was crying piteously, complaining of the *perdicion* of his child, but no news had ever been heard. She had heard the same complaint from a couple named Aisé or d'Aysée. She had also heard of the loss of many other infants in Brittany, of which great complaint had been made; that seven alone had been lost from Tiffauges; that they had all been taken from the fields while guarding the cattle, and no one knew what had become of them or what to do about finding them.

Macé Sorin and his wife recount the loss of several of the foregoing, of whom nothing had ever been heard, and that it was presumed that they had been taken by the English for the ransom and deliverance of Michel de Sillé, prisoner.

Perrine, the wife of Clemens Rondeau, of Machecoul, declared that Monsieur François Prelati, and the Marquis de Ceva, while part of the retinue of the Baron de Retz, were lodged in a chamber of her house; that she heard the Marquis say to François that he had found a handsome page at Dieppe, at which François was joyful; that the page came to live with the said François, and was there for about fifteen days. Upon her demand of François as to where the boy had gone, and what had become of him, François responded that he had been deceived in him and had sent him away. That François and Eustache Blanchet also occupied another small house in the neighbourhood belonging to Perrot Cahn; that on the descent of Jean l'Abbé there had been found in the chamber the powdered bones of an infant, or infants, and she had seen an infant's bloody chemise, which gave forth a bad odour.

André Brechet, of the Parish of Saint Croix de Machecoul, says that about a year and half before he was a watchman, or was watching at the castle of Machecoul, and after midnight he fell asleep; he was awakened by a contest on the wall in which a large man had his naked dagger, and said to the little one by his side, "You are dead" (*Tu est mort*); that he, the witness, was filled with great fear and quietly escaped.

Ysabeau, wife of Guillaume Hamelin, makes oath that about seven days before the end of the past year, she sent her two sons—one fifteen years, the other seven, or thereabouts—to the town of Machecoul to purchase bread, giving them the money therefor; that they never returned, and she has never had any news of or from them. She reports having heard a similar story from Micheau Bouer and his wife, who had also lost one of their infants, who had never since been seen. She was supported in the testimony of her loss by Perrot Pasqueteau, Jehan Soreau, Katerine de Grepie, Guillaume Garnier, Perrine wife of Jehan Caeffin, Jehanne wife of Estienne Landays, and Perrot Soudan.

Guillemete, wife of Micheau Bouer, declares upon her oath that seven days after Easter last, her son of eight years, a beautiful white infant, *bel enffant et blanc*, went to Machecoul; that he never returned and they have never received any news, however many searches she and her husband have made. That on the day after they had given charity at Machecoul for the deceased Mahé Le Breton, she, who was guarding the cattle as they grazed, was approached by a large man, in black, who, among other things, asked of her where were the children who usually guarded the cattle. She said that they had gone to Machecoul, when he departed in that direction.

Guillaume Rodigo, living at Bourgneuf-en-Rais, testifies to the loss of his apprentice, aged fifteen years. Marguerite Sorin, chambermaid for Rodigo, tells how, as she and the boy were playing some games together in the house after supper, Poitou came and, taking the boy apart, talked to him in a low voice. On his departure she interrogated the boy as to what was said, but he refused to tell. Soon after he left the house in his doublet without saying where he was going. Since then she has never seen him or heard any news of him. They were supported by Guillaume Plumet and his wife, and Michel Gerart.

Thomas Aysée and his wife, living at Machecoul, declare that at the last fête of Pentecost they sent their son of ten years to ask alms at the castle, and that they have never seen their son since; he has never returned. They heard, from a girl, that she had seen the son at the château, along with others who were also asking alms; that alms were given first to the girls and then to the boys; that this girl said she had heard one of the men of the castle say to this boy that he had not had any meat (that is, to eat), and invite him into the castle to be fed, whereupon both entered and the boy was seen no more.

Jannette, the wife of Eucasse (Eustache?) Douret, of Saint Ligier, declares on oath that about fifteen days before Christmas last, having heard that the Baron de Retz would give alms, according to the custom in her own town, she sent her two boys, one of ten years, the other of seven, and though some of her neighbours had seen them on the way, and at the town of Machecoul, she had never seen them since, and although she and her husband had made every search, they had obtained no news.

October 2, 1440.

Jehan de Grepie, Regnaud Donété, of the parish of Notre Dame of Nantes, says under oath, that about Saint John's day, two years past, she lost a child of about twelve years while on his way to school, and since then she had never seen him. The only news had been that Perrine Martin, a prisoner in Nantes, had confessed that she had taken the said child to the Baron de Retz in his chamber, at his Hôtel de la Suze in Nantes; that the said Baron had commanded her to take the child to Machecoul and deliver him to the porter, and this she had done. That she had heard Jean Hubert and Denis de Lemyon, acquaintances of his, complain each one of having lost a son; that at the time of the loss of his son, Gilles de Retz was at his Hôtel de la Suze in Nantes, and that the said Perrine lived near him. The witness made complaint to various of the servants and followers of Gilles at his said house (Hôtel de la Suze) and she was always told that they thought his son had gone to Machecoul to become a page.

Jean Jenvret and his wife, of Nantes, declare their loss of a son of nine years in the same way, and by the same person as told by Donété.

Jean Hubert and his wife, of Saint Leonart, in Nantes, declare that on Thursday after Saint John's day last, two years ago, they lost their son, fourteen years of age; that he made the acquaintance of some of the men servants, or followers of Gilles de Retz; that he talked with his mother of the promises they had made if he would enter the service with them. He recounted how he had seen the Baron de Retz in his chamber and waited upon him, for which he had received a present of some cake which he had brought to his mother; that after his permanent entry into the service of the Baron, and his departure from Nantes, they had never seen or heard of him more.

Agaice, wife of Denis de Lemion, says that about a year and a half before, her nephew of the age of eighteen years, who frequented the Hôtel de la Suze, where resided the Baron de Retz, was approached by one of his men, or servants, with an offer to enter the service of the Baron, which he did, and has never returned or been heard of since.

Jehanne, wife of Guibelet Delit, declares that during the Easter holidays, she lost a child of seven years; that he frequented la Suze, where a man named Cherpy had persuaded him to join the service of the Baron de Retz. This done, she had never seen or had news of her child.

Jehan Toutblanc, of Saint Étienne de Montluc, records that at

Saint Julian a year ago, on departing from his house, he left it in charge of a young ward of fourteen years, named Jean also, for whom he was tutor. On his return from his journey, he could not find the boy, has never seen him, nor heard any news from him.

Jean Fougere, of Saint Donacien, near Nantes, records that about two years since he lost his son of twelve years, a well-favoured boy, and that since that time he has had no news as to what became of him.

Jean Ferot, Guillaume Jacob, Perrin Blanchet, Thomas Beauvis, Eonnet Jehan, Denis de Lemyon, of the parish of Notre Dame, of Nantes, record under their oaths, their knowledge concerning the loss of the sons of Jean Hubert, Régnaud Donété, and Guillaume Avril, that complaints and public clamour have been heard by these witnesses for two years and a half; that for one year past it has been commonly said that the Baron de Retz abducts infants in order to slay them.

Nicole, wife of Vincent Bonnereau; Philipe, wife of Mathis Ernaut; Jehanne, wife of Guillaume Prieur, all of the parish of Saint Croix of Nantes, support the claim of Jean Jenvret and his wife as to the loss of their son of nine years, and that for a year and a half they have heard by common report that *le sire de Retz* and his men capture and kill small children. They have also heard of the loss of the young son of Eonnet de Villeblanche, and that for three months past he has not been seen in his neighbourhood nor heard from.

October 6, 1440.

Jean Estaisse and Michele, his wife, testify to the loss of a boy of the age of eleven years named Perrot Dagaie. Relate the notoriety of the rumour that the Baron de Retz and his men capture and kill infants.

Jean Chiquet, parchment-maker, testifies to the evil reputation of the Baron de Retz and his men in abducting children.

Pierre Badieu, cloth merchant of Chanteloup, testifies to the abduction of two children aged about nine years, the infants of Robin Pavot.

Jean Darel describes his son, who, while the father was sick in bed, was captured in the Rue du Mercheil, where he was playing with other children; that he has no knowledge by whom or where he was taken; that he has never seen or heard of him since.

Jehanne, wife of Darel, says that on the day of Saint Père (or Pierre) June 29th, one year ago, there was abducted from her place in the city of Nantes, her son, Olivier, seven or eight years of age, since which time she has never seen him nor had any news of him. Her mother describes the abduction by saying that she was coming from vespers, leading the child; that near the church of Saint Saturnine, when in the crowd, somebody made away with the child; that she and all his relatives sought for him in every direction, but they have never seen or heard of him since.

Eonnette, wife of Jean Bremant, supports the foregoing witnesses as to the abduction of Olivier.

Nichole, wife of Jean Hubert, of the parish of Saint Vincent, had a son named Jean of fourteen years of age, who was lost or abducted as described by her husband aforesaid. She sustains him in his testimony.

Jean Bureau and his wife, Johanne, Thebault Geoffroi and her daughter, and Guillaume Hemeri, support the claim of the abduction of the Hubert child.

De la Grepie, Régnaud Donété, Jean Ferot and his wife, Pierres Blanchett, and Guillaume Jacob, all support the claim of the abduction of the apprentice, Donété, heretofore described.